Young Brides, Old Treasures:
MACEDONIAN EMBROIDERED DRESS

BOBBIE SUMBERG, EDITOR

Museum of International Folk Art and the Macedonian Arts Council

This book is published in conjunction with an exhibition of the same
name, produced by the Museum of
International Folk Art in collabo-
ration with the Macedonian Arts
Council.

© Museum of International Folk
Art

Bobbie Sumberg, editor
Photographs by Addison Doty

Distributed by the:
University of Washington Press
P.O. Box 50096, Seattle WA 98145
U.S.A.
www.washington.edu/uwpress

Staro Kupuvam (*I Buy Old Things*)
ACO SHOPOV

Eh, da znaesh, kalesh Kalina,

Tokmi se tokmi mlada nevesta,

Ke ti se zablazi . . .

Eh stari rizi, mladi nevesti,

Prekrasni nosii.

If you only knew, dark-eyed Kalina,

Go ahead and be a young bride,

You'll be in bliss . . .

Ah, old treasures for young brides,

Splendid folk costumes.

Contents

Ohrid

Foreword

THE MUSEUM OF INTERNATIONAL FOLK ART now houses the largest, most comprehensive collection of complete Macedonian folk outfits with jewelry in the United States because of a multiyear relationship between a curator, a private nonprofit organization, and two extraordinary collectors. The unique partnership between the Macedonian Arts Council and the Museum of International Folk Art has resulted in this publication and an exhibition of the Museum's holdings from this fascinating corner of Europe. Very little has been published, outside of the Republic of Macedonia, about the material culture in this part of the world, thus making this project a ground-breaking endeavor. Within these pages, you will see, probably for the first time, the full range of these breathtaking ensembles, a visual testimony to the needlework skills passed through generations of Macedonian women, who invested their creations with love for the family members that would be wearing these fineries on special village occasions.

The Museum of International Folk Art has been a home to extraordinary examples of European folk dress since 1953, when its founder, Florence Dibell Bartlett, donated complete ensembles, which she had collected in the first half of the twentieth century, from Hungary, Slovakia, Sweden, Norway, Greece, Spain, and other sojourns. Jewelry from Macedonia formed a part of this initial collection. Bartlett's generosity inspired other donors to add to this collection of textiles and costumes, which now numbers some 20,000 pieces, making it the largest ethnographic textile and costume collection in the United States.

Since 2002, when Pavlina Proevska, Executive Director of the Macedonian Arts Council, requested a meeting with the Museum's Curator of Textiles and Costume, Dr. Bobbie Sumberg embraced the project, recognizing that here was an opportunity, working in concert with the Macedonian Arts Council and scholars and curators in Macedonia, to open the door for the American public to witness some of the most extraordinary village dress in the world.

It has been a great pleasure to work with the Executive Director of the Macedonian Arts Council, Pavlina Proevska, who is the inspiration for this worthy project.

MARSHA C. BOL, PH.D.
Director
Museum of International Folk Art

Skopsa Crna Gora

Preface

ONE OF THE GREAT, if lesser-known, Macedonian heroes was not a revolutionary but a protector of culture. A simple tailor, born in the city of Prilep in 1829, Marko Cepenkov was the first and most prolific documenter of Macedonian folk life. He recorded everything he heard–stories, songs, riddles, dreams and their interpretations, magic incantations, children's games, pledges, curses, blessings, beliefs, customs, and descriptions of crafts and musical instruments. While he did not collect folk costumes, he did collect the stories behind the costumes in this book, and it is in his spirit that they have been brought together for this collection. Busy fending off the cultural assimilation of generations of outside invaders, the Macedonians have had little time for the documentation of their cultural heritage. It is only in the last sixty years that this process has begun in earnest. With this collection the Macedonian Arts Council has joined in that effort to affirm and preserve Macedonia's cultural past.

Imagine the road these costumes have traveled.

They were born in the hands of young girls, embroidering countless stitches on long winter nights, transferring their hopes and dreams into the exquisite patterns of their bridal dresses, into the multi-colored edges of the sleeves, the silver-threaded woven strands of the outside vests, the pompoms that adorned the head scarves.

How far those hopes and dreams have come, to find in an internationally-renowned museum a permanent home for what they have created; a testament to the creativity, passion, and persistence of the Macedonian woman.

Those who have donated these items, others involved in securing them, and those who have welcomed them have all joined hands in an endeavor begun long ago to preserve Macedonian cultural riches by documenting them and making them available to a wider audience through this book and the accompanying exhibition.

To glimpse the micro-culture of Macedonia is to begin a life-long love, like that of the little tailor from Prilep who must be smiling at us from above.

PAVLINA PROEVSKA
Executive Director
Macedonian Arts Council

Acknowledgements

THIS BOOK IS PART OF A LARGER PROJECT on Macedonian dress that was begun in 2002, when Pavlina Proevska, Executive Director of the Macedonian Arts Council in New York City, arrived in Santa Fe with an idea. It was formalized in 2006 by the Museum of International Folk Art's previous director, Dr. Joyce Ice, with a letter confirming the museum's commitment to working with the council to collect and exhibit Macedonian dress. Since then, work has proceeded on many fronts to realize the plan developed by Ms. Proevska to place a significant group of Macedonian dress elements in a US museum where they would be preserved, shown, and available for future research. Dr. Marsha Bol, director of the museum, has provided her full support to the project. Although it was already in place when she assumed leadership of the institution, her realization of the importance of the subject, her appreciation of the material's appeal, and her assistance has allowed us to assemble the largest and most comprehensive collection of Macedonian dress in the country.

The two major donors, Ronald Wixman and Bernard Ziobro, were essential to the success of both this catalog and the exhibition, not only by donating their collections, but also by acting as translators during the photography contained inside, and assisting with dressing the mannequins. Marge Gajicki offered her time and language expertise to the project, creating a smooth beginning to the photography session with her calm presence. Dedicated textile collection volunteers Sally Brewer, Barbara Forslund, and Ava Fullerton worked overtime to facilitate the project; Ruth LaNore, our assistant curator, provided able assistance that helped everything be on time and well organized.

Vladimir Janevski was crucial to the quality and accuracy of this catalog. He not only contributed to this book, but also spent two weeks in Santa Fe organizing the component parts of the ensembles, dressing the mannequins, providing information on provenance and use, and explaining some of the complexity of Macedonian women's dress. Without his expertise, the photographs in the book would not have been accurate and there would be a lot less information in the captions. As always, it was a pleasure to work with Addison Doty in the photo studio.

In Macedonia thanks go to Jone Eftimovski and Blagorodna Josifovska, who provided some of the pieces in the MOIFA collection, and to the staff at the Museum of Macedonia for authorizing their export. Natasha Boshkovska in Skopje translated two of the four chapters written in Macedonian, going beyond her official capacity as translator to facilitate communication with the authors. Of the other two chapters, one was translated by Pavlina Proevska and the other by Bernard Ziobro, who helped with numerous language questions and the glossary.

Funding for this catalog was provided by the International Folk Art Foundation, the Museum of New Mexico Foundation, and by a donation from R. L. Shep. The Macedonian Arts Council provided funds for printing and for my first trip to Macedonia in 2008.

Meeting Pavlina in 2002 started me on a journey I never anticipated taking. Her knowledge, enthusiasm, and persistence, both as director of the Arts Council and personally, to expose her country's unique and little known culture to the world, have helped carry this project through the years to a successful completion. Through my time spent with Pavlina and intensive study of the history of Macedonia, as well as deep scrutiny of the museum collection as donations arrived, I have not only learned about a part of the world and a textile tradition that was unknown to me but have made a fast friend.

Over the last few years I have developed a profound appreciation for the pieces and the women who made them. It is a mistake to value these garments as textile art alone; they cannot be separated from their makers – the village women of Macedonia. The legacy of their hands and minds will live on in the museum and in this volume for future generations to admire.

Near Kumanovo

Introduction

BOBBIE SUMBERG

MACEDONIAN ETHNIC DRESS has it all. Not only is it full of meaning and significance, it is visually stunning, quite possibly overwhelming, and embodies the skills, expectations, hopes and fears, creative use of materials, and aesthetic sense of the individuals who made and wore it. Saturated with cultural meaning, these many-layered ensembles rank among the best examples of textile art anywhere. For more than fifty years, the Museum of International Folk Art has been assembling a collection of dress worn by the Orthodox Christian villagers of Macedonia primarily from the period of 1890–1950. We are proud to present it in this volume, which combines outstanding images with the best scholarship written by Macedonian experts offered here in English for the first time. We hope this catalog will spur further studies in the field as well as inspire the general reader to get out the atlas and become more familiar with this vital region of the world.

Political and Geographic Macedonia: Changing Borders

Archaeological evidence shows that the land area of today's Republic of Macedonia,[1] in the center of the Balkan Peninsula, has been inhabited at least since the Neolithic Age. The remains of several settlements that were inhabited from c. 6400 BC to c. 5000 BC have been excavated at Anza-Begovo, Porodin, Zelenikovo, and Vrshnik, producing painted pottery, figurines, ornaments, and tools.[2] Although there are large gaps in the archaeological record, human habitation has been constant since then. It has been argued that the people in this region developed a distinct identity during the Early Iron Age (c. 1050–650 BC), differing from that of the Illyrians to the west, the Thracians to the northeast, and the Greeks to the south.[3] Migration, conflict, conquest, and reverse characterized the next several centuries—the period of empire-building begun by King Perdiccas I, extended by

---

[1]   As of the spring of 2011, the name "Republic of Macedonia" is still disputed by the Republic of Greece. At all times in this book, "Macedonia" refers to the land area that was a former republic of Yugoslavia and established itself as an independent country in 1991.

[2]   Marija Gimbutas,"Excavation at Anza, Macedonia," *Archaeology 25,* 2 (1972): 112–123.

[3]   Andrew Rossos, *Macedonia and the Macedonians: A History* (Stanford University: Hoover Institution Press, 2008), 11.

Philip II, and reaching its greatest extent with Alexander III.[4] The Romans conquered Macedonia in 168 BC and ruled over the region; when the empire was split in 395, Macedonia and the rest of the Balkan Peninsula became part of the eastern Roman or Byzantine Empire.

The Goths invaded over the course of the third to fifth centuries; the Huns followed suit in the fourth and fifth centuries. Slavic people coming from the northeast began arriving in the sixth century and stayed, assimilating those people already in place. Until the twenty-first century, Slavic-speaking Macedonians remain the majority of the population, and various other peoples make up minorities. Vlachs, who speak a language related to Romanian, are the descendants of those original inhabitants who were not assimilated by the Slavs.[5] Roma arrived and settled in Macedonia some time in the eleventh century, fleeing the Seljuk invasion of Armenia.[6] A large Sephardic Jewish population grew up around Monastir (also called Bitola) after their expulsion from Spain in 1492, while other Jews lived in the region since Roman times.[7] Turks and small numbers of other minorities arrived with the Ottoman Empire, which encouraged Albanians to settle in villages on the western edge of the present-day borders, as well as in the city of Skopje, beginning in the eighteenth century. [8]

Another constant in the history of this area has been conflict over who controlled the land and the people living there. Macedonia belonged to the Byzantine Empire from 395, the first Bulgarian Empire from 864–971, and the empire of Tsar Samuil from 971–1018. At that point, Constantinople (the capital of the Byzantine Empire) regained control of the territory and held on, despite deteriorating conditions and occasional loss of control over parts of the region, until 1204. The next two centuries of warfare and shifting military domination, which gave Macedonia at various times to the Kingdom of Serbia, the Empire of Bulgaria, the Byzantine Empire, and the Kingdom of Salonika, finally ended in 1400 with capitulation to the Ottomans, who hung on until the early twentieth century. Macedonia was the last European territory of the Ottoman Empire to be relinquished, in 1913 at the conclusion of the first Balkan War.

At this point, the territory that today constitutes the Republic of Macedonia was given to the Kingdom of the Serbs, Croats, and Slovenes in the Treaty of Bucharest and proclaimed to be South Serbia,[9] which it remained until 1944 when the land and the people on it joined the Socialist Federal Republic of Yugoslavia as the People's Republic of Macedonia. Following the breakup of Yugoslavia and a

---

4   My intention here is not to claim Alexander III, known as the Great, as a direct ancestor of the present day Macedonians but to trace the history of invasion and influence in the region and demonstrate the multicultural aspect of Macedonia through time as well as possible influences on dress in the region.

5   Rossos, *Macedonia,* 24.

6   Maria Koinova, "Roma of Macedonia," (Center for Documentation and Information on Minorities in Europe – Southeast Europe, 2000).

7   F. H. Colson, Philo. *The Embassy to Gaius* (Cambridge; London: Harvard University Press, 1962). The first synagogue in Macedonia is found in the ruins of Stobi, built in the second century.

8   N. Anastasovski, "Contestations over Macedonian Identity, 1870–1912" (Ph.D. diss., Melbourne: Victoria University, 2005), 117.

9   Rossos, *Macedonia,* 131.

referendum held on September 8, 1991, the Republic of Macedonia declared itself a sovereign nation.[10]

Cultural Macedonia: The Centrality of Women, Dress, and Identity

"Social inferiority of women is one of the basic themes of this culture," Joseph Obrebski noted in the 1930s.[11] Macedonian society was heavily male dominated until recent times. Brides lived with their husbands' families and were expected to do the heaviest share of the work. Yet women were also responsible for the cycle of religious ritual performance that was vital to the well-being of the family and by extension, the village, including the mortuary and post-mortuary rites that reinforced the kinship ties of the married couple. The headwoman, the wife of the headman and mother of the married sons in the household, directed the work of her daughters-in-law. She herself was ultimately responsible for the religious observations required for the family well-being. Religious activity was dominated by women who were considered inferior and incompetent in the secular realm, which was dominated by men. This division of responsibility helped to restore balance within the conflict-filled living situation of father and brothers in a single household. By tending to the dead of their in-laws as well as of their birth family, women maintained the link not only among families but also between present and past, as represented by the dead.[12] Women and their labor created the fabric of society through the maintenance of the living and the commemoration of the dead.

The production of clothing was an essential aspect of women's work in village Macedonia. When one sees the elaborate embroidery and multiple garments worn by a bride, it must be appreciated that the majority of the materials (linen, cotton, and wool) were grown and then processed at home by the same women who manufactured the garments and then decorated them. This labor took place while raising the children, cooking and cleaning, tending the garden plot, helping in the fields at planting and harvest time, and providing clothing for children and husbands. The time, energy, and expertise required boggle the mind. In some villages, all adult men left for seasonal or long-term work, leaving the women to oversee the flocks and the fields in addition to all their other responsibilities.

The richness of the dress shown in these pages belies the marginal living conditions in the villages of Macedonia at the turn of the twentieth century. Many people lived in poverty, in small houses with dirt floors and open hearths. Photos show horse drawn carts in use late into the twentieth century. Life was a cycle of hard work interspersed with periods of ritual religious activity that culminated in feasting and dancing. The clothing that was made and worn was intimately related to this cycle both by rituals that inaugurated weaving and embroidery (see the

---

10   This necessarily brief and inadequate summary of the political status of Macedonia deliberately avoids any explication of how borders and boundaries were disputed amongst Greece, Bulgaria, Albania, and Serbia. Along with territorial disputes there was a concerted effort, often coercive, among all parties to garner the loyalty and support of the people of Macedonia, whose nationality changed as their ruling power changed.

11   Tanas Vrashinovski, ed. *Joseph Obrebski: Macedonian Poreche 1932–1933* (Prilep and Skopje: Institute for Slavonic Culture and Matica, 2003), 85.

12   Ibid., 90.

Techniques and Materials of Production chapter in this book) and by prohibitions, *zarotsi,* placed on work and diet, among other things, that applied during the holy periods of a village's religious calendar.[13]

Making and wearing clothing are cultural activities. The most ancient element of Macedonian women's dress, the long shirt-like chemise that is thought to have originated with the ancient Slavs, long served as a canvas of culture. Certain stitches, motifs, color combinations, and the placement of embroidery on the chemise became associated with specific groups in a process that might be called "cultural selection." One village cluster chose red-dyed wool for embroidery, while another preferred dark blue. One group might develop a particular embroidery stitch that differed from the stitches used by their neighbors. Over time, these choices coalesced into recognizable styles associated with an ethnic group or a specific village. A sense of congruence and ownership grew between the maker and her creation. The formalizing of these choices resulted in a kind of boundary—this is ours and not yours; we are us and not you—that served to identify a person as insider or outsider.

Women living in the villages of Macedonia created a visual system of meaning drawing on techniques, colors, motifs, and garment types. The meaning system reflected their society's agreement about gender roles; for example, women were expected to work hard, to bear healthy children–especially males, to clothe the family, and to use their skills in their assigned realm of home and farm. Clothing also expressed Macedonians' beliefs about how to protect themselves from danger by calling on the magical properties of materials, such as silver, and color, such as red. Through the years, people gradually forgot the original impulses that guided their choices, so when asked why this color, this stitch, this shape, the answer was, "Because this is how we do it." The form still conveyed identity.

In village Macedonia, until World War II, dress communicated identity on several different levels. Ethnicity, whether Orthodox Macedonian,[14] Vlach, Albanian, or Roma, could be discerned through dress. Religious affiliation, especially Orthodox Christians and Muslims, could be broadly distinguished through dress. For instance, only Christians are said to have had small cross forms embroidered onto the chemise or head scarf. Macedonian Muslims, who lived on the Albanian border in the area of Golo Brdo, dressed differently than neighboring Albanian Muslims and Christian Orthodox Macedonians.[15] Within the Orthodox community, the focus of this book, details of dress indicated which region or even which village a person came from (see The Embroidery on Macedonian Traditional Dress chapter in this book). There were also distinctions based on "tribal" identities, such as Miyak and Brsyak that tended to coincide with region.

An even more distinctive aspect of identity shown through dress was gender. Although in some areas men and women might wear a similar form of outer garment,

13   Joseph Obrebski, Joel Halpern, and Barbara Halpern, *Ritual and Social Structure in a Macedonian Village,* Research Report 16, Anthropology Research Reports series (1977). Access at http://scholarworks.umass.edu.

14   In Macedonia, ethnic identity is heavily influenced by and related to religion, a survival of the Ottoman Empire's emphasis on rule by religion.

15   G. Zdravev, *Macedonian Folk Costumes* (Skopje: Matica Makedonska, 2005), 96–101.

otherwise the dress of adult men and women was very different. Men wore trousers of some sort, made from home-produced heavy wool or cotton, while Orthodox women wore the long shirt or shift called a chemise (*koshula*) as the basic garment. Muslim and Roma women wore trousers but of a very different cut and fabric than those of men. Children up to age three were dressed alike; at that point they donned gendered dress. Each stage of a female's life, from puberty to marriage to the birth of the first child to old age, was marked by changes in what she wore and how it was decorated. Within the categories determined by age or marital and maternal status, dress for everyday, special occasions, and rituals also varied. Insiders who knew the relevant signs and symbols could read village dress.

Differences between urban and rural people were also noticeable. From 1400 to 1913, the upper echelon of urban society consisted of officials of the Ottoman regime and wealthy merchants. The rich emulated Ottoman style, incorporating expensive imported fabrics and materials, while village residents made their clothing from home-produced materials. Some elements of clothing, such as the *pafta* or silver belt buckle, were worn by women in all levels of society for special occasions. In the city of Bitola, known as Monastir during the Ottoman period, people lived in close proximity with others of different nationalities wearing fashionable, cosmopolitan dress that sometimes incorporated ethnic identifiers. In 1937 Rebecca West noted a Sephardic woman dressed in "a close cap rimmed with gold sequins and a purple gown of seventeenth-century Spanish fashion"[16] entering a home. Thus, both urban and rural people's dress in Macedonia served several identifying functions.

Changing Macedonia: Disappearing Dress

Although no longer made or worn in the twenty-first century, people in many parts of Macedonia wore distinctive village dress daily into the 1950s. It seems to have reached its fullest expression in the last half of the nineteenth century,[17] which was, astoundingly enough, a most unsettled time politically. The Ottomans were fighting to retain control over their European territories while Serbian, Bulgarian, and Macedonian nationalists sought to wrest that control from them. Rural people experienced varying levels of violence on a regular basis, ranging from tax extortion to rape and massacre of entire villages. Travel was fraught with difficulty because of the embattled Ottoman local administration, its military irregulars known as *bashi buzuks,* bandits, and political partisans, each of which sought to maximize its own situation at the expense of the villagers.

Political unrest can precipitate social change. People move about during war. The fighting forces go wherever battle takes them, and some soldiers stay on after a war ends. Civilians migrate temporarily or permanently to avoid the conflict or are moved about by rulers for their own purposes. Highly differentiated groups of people come into contact, for better or worse. The introduction of new genes, ideas, and material goods almost always results.

---

16   Rebecca West, *Black Lamb and Grey Falcon* (New York: The Viking Press, 1941; New York: Penguin, 2007), 777.

17   Zdravev. *Macedonian Folk Costumes,* 10.

On the other hand, difficult conditions can encourage the conservation of traditional forms of art. Under the Ottomans, the peasants of Macedonia paid their taxes in scarce cash and agricultural produce. Their contact with the cosmopolitan administration of the empire was very limited; they were left in their mountain villages to live and worship as they could, while developing a strong antagonism to everything Turkish. Ruth Trouton describes the communally organized extended family, known as *zadruga* throughout the Balkans, including Macedonia, as the site of the most intensive production of weaving and embroidery. In the largest zadrugas, labor was organized to take advantage of available resources, including women's ability with loom and needle, subsequently encouraging the development of these arts.[18]

The developing revolutionary climate and nationalist political organizations of the first few years of the twentieth century seemed to have an effect as well. Keith Brown writes, "In 1905, reportedly as part of his progressive agenda, the *vojvoda* [revolutionary leader] Jane Sandanski forbade the wearing of jewelry at weddings."[19] In 1903 the British consul McGregor observed that Macedonian peasant women were selling their jewelry to equip their men with rifles to fight the Turks.[20]

A common reason cited for the long life of local dress practices in rural Macedonia is the isolated nature of the villages. In mountainous areas severe winter weather could cut off access by road, when there was one, or footpath, leaving villagers to themselves to develop their arts. Young women were confined to the house, especially during the late Ottoman period, to protect them from the danger of contact with foreign occupying forces.[21] At the same time, men from these isolated villages, where agricultural land was scarce—making it very hard to support a family—had a history of migrating to urban areas to work for periods of time. During the nineteenth century Macedonian men went to Serbia, Bulgaria, and Romania for two to three years or more at a time.[22] At the beginning of the twentieth century, they began going to Canada and the United States as well. In March 1906, 600 men left for the United States in one day.[23] They often stayed away for five years at a time, returning home to marry and to visit for a few months during the summer. The money they sent sustained their families still living in the village.

Far from producing a uniform outcome, the effects of migration differed from place to place.[24] One possibility was an elaboration of existing forms, here described in the field notes of two anthropologists during their first visit to Macedonia in 1954.

---

[18] Ruth Trouton, *Peasant Renaissance in Yugoslavia 1900–1950* (London: Routledge and Kegan Paul Ltd, 1952; Westport, CT: Greenwood, 1973).

[19] Keith Brown, *The Past in Question: Modern Macedonia and the Uncertainties of Nation* (Princeton, NJ: Princeton University, 2003), 275, fn 15.

[20] Ibid.

[21] Olive Lodge, *Peasant Life in Jugoslavia* (London: Seeley, Servie and Co. Ltd., 1941), 95 fn 1.

[22] Joel Halpern, "The Pechalba Tradition in Macedonia, a Case Study." 1975. Available at: http://works.bepress.com/joel_halpern/86

[23] Gregory Michaelidis, "Salvation Abroad: Macedonian Migration to North America and the Making of Modern Macedonia, 1870–1970" (Ph.D. diss., University of Maryland, 2005).

[24] This section is based on very incomplete data because little has been published. I include it to suggest the complexities and encourage more research.

About 1900 the men from this area [Galichnik] started leaving their village to seek work elsewhere. They sent money home and once every five years or so they would return for half a year. Afterwards he would leave his wife and family again. Gradually, with the combination of money sent home, and with the sheep providing plenty of good wool, the women's costumes became more elaborate and were increasingly embellished with gold and silver. They used the traditional one hundred silver filigree buttons, along with imported silk from Czechoslovakia. This resulted in lavish wool fabrics incorporating fringe and trims.[25]

Another possibility was the gradual or abrupt abandonment of local dress. By the 1930s only old men in Galichnik wore the long pleated coat called *dolama*, one of several elements of local dress, but photos of the times show some men in the typical trousers, sash, and shirt of the area and others in suits and overcoats. Women who lived in the village wore their local style, while girls who had moved to the city and wore cosmopolitan dress there, dressed in fine Galichnik style when they came back for festivals and their weddings.[26] Today, the village is deserted most of the year, repopulated only in July for the Galichnik Wedding Festival, a re-enactment of what was once a vital aspect of village life, the time when sojourning young men returned home and married.

Many factors contributed to changes in the production and use of dress in the villages during the twentieth century. Trouton noted the breakup of the zadruga in Macedonia in the 1930s and the concomitant loss of women's labor and expertise: "Similarly, the more elaborate types of weaving and embroidery tended to disappear [with the disappearance of the zadruga], because in the small household the women were too busy to devote so much time to it."[27] While visiting Bitola in 1937, Rebecca West bought embroidered chemises from women who made them for newly urbanized villagers who had come there to work and didn't have the time or materials to make their own clothing.[28] Industrialization and urbanization during the Socialist Federal Republic of Yugoslavia period (1943–1991) changed the population of the country from 63% involved in agriculture in 1953 to 15% in 1991.[29] Development of infrastructure and industrial capacity led to a more modern lifestyle, one that did not emphasize the craft traditions over formal education. Thus the switch from village to cosmopolitan dress happened in different places at different times for different reasons.

Macedonia in the Museum of International Folk Art: A Growing Collection

When the Museum of International Folk Art opened its doors in 1953, there were nine items from the Debar region of Macedonia in the collection. Several of these

---

25   Joel M. Halpern, and Barbara K. Halpern, "Letters from Macedonia" EthnoAnthropoZoom, (2003). Available at: http://works.bepress.com/joel_halpern/8

26   Olive Lodge, "Serbian Wedding Customs: St. Peter's Day in Galichnik," The Slavonic and East European Review, 13, no. 39 (1935): 650– 673.

27   Trouton, *Peasant Renaissance*, 85.

28   West, *Black Lamb and Grey Falcon*, 782.

29   Rossos, *Macedonia*, 249.

were displayed in the inaugural exhibition from 1953–1956 and later in the World of Folk Costume exhibition in 1971. Eight of these nine were collected in Monastir (Bitola) by Evelyn Richards and authenticated by the Serbian ethnographer Dr. Milenko Filipovic. Thirty additional pieces were purchased by the International Folk Art Foundation (IFAF) from 1969–1972, and nine items of dress were donated in 1978 by Mrs. Frank Hibben who had collected them in Macedonia in 1938.

There was a hiatus in collecting until the mid-1990s when IFAF again made purchases through a Santa Fe researcher while she was in Skopje. In 2002 an initial meeting with Pavlina Proevska, the Executive Director of the New York-based Macedonian Arts Council, jump-started a new collecting effort and plans for an exhibition. In 2005, the first donation through the Macedonian Arts Council came to the museum: an ensemble from Mariovo donated by Ms. Sheila Krstevski. Soon after, the Council initiated discussions with Dr. Ronald Wixman. After a few years of discussion he decided, in 2008, to donate most of his collection to the museum through the Arts Council. Ron began traveling to Macedonia and other parts of the Balkan Peninsula in the early 1960s with his partner and fellow folk dancer Stephen Glaser. Unusually, and luckily for the museum, when possible they collected complete outfits from villagers and antiques dealers, including jewelry, socks, and head scarves. In 2008 and 2009, Ron donated 121 pieces of Macedonian dress.

In 2010, Bernard Ziobro donated 145 dress components through the Macedonian Arts Council. Lt. Col. B.W. Ziobro USMC Ret. lived in Beograd (Belgrade), Yugoslavia, from January 1971 to June 1973, while on active duty with the United States Marine Corps at the American embassy. During that time he made multiple trips to Macedonian cities, towns, and villages where he acquired the majority of his collection, later exchanging with other collectors to acquire missing pieces. Meanwhile, I made two trips to Macedonia for the museum in 2008 and 2010 and we acquired two sets of clothing, from Gorna Reka and most of the Karaguni Vlach ensemble, and multiple pieces of jewelry. Mr. and Mrs. William Hennessy generously funded the acquisition of the Gorna Prespa ensemble, Mr. Mike Zafirovski donated several pieces of jewelry, and Mr. Donald Berlanti provided the funds for the Ovche Pole ensemble, while Mr. DeWitt Mallary and Ms. Sharon Sharpe both donated rare head pieces. Three passionate collectors in Macedonia, two amateur and the other a scholar, donated numerous items through the efforts of the Macedonian Arts Council in Macedonia. Ms. Blagorodna Josifovska donated ten pieces; Mr. Jone Eftimovski gave several items; and Professor Vladimir Janevski another nine pieces. By concentrating on acquiring sets of clothing as complete as possible, the museum has assembled a unique and valuable resource of 485 pieces for display and study in the future.

Macedonia is a multiethnic, multireligious society, as presented in this book by Davorin Trpeski. This volume and the exhibition of the same name shows dress of Orthodox Christian Macedonians only while acknowledging the existence of several other dress traditions. Reasons for this include space considerations, as well as the interests of the collector/donors whose collections we have in the museum in 2011. The museum hopes to continue collecting; especially pieces that represent additional communities as well as pieces from other areas of geographic Macedonia in order to fully represent the diverse ethnography of Macedonia.

This volume brings together Macedonian authors in translation with an American museum collection; presenting new information in English as well as an overview of the dress tradition of the different regions. Angelina Krsteva has written extensively about Macedonian embroidery, both generally and in several monographs on particular regions. Her chapter focuses in great detail on embroidery of the Miyaks, much of which has never been published before. Davorin Trpeski illuminates the complexities of the ethnic landscape at the turn of the twentieth century in his work for this volume while the authors Jasemin Nazim, Sanja Dimovska, Tatjana Gjogjiovska, and Slavica Hristova, all museum curators, present the technical aspects of how these sumptuous ensembles were made. Vladimir Janevski introduces the topic of hair dressing with a detailed description of one village's tradition. The catalog is organized by geographical region. Thus, the dress of Miyaks who migrated to the Middle Vardar and Brsyak regions are shown in those sections rather than with the other Miyak groups. We hope this volume adds to the reader's knowledge and enjoyment of the pieces presented as well as adding to the scholarship on the topic of ethnic dress in general and Macedonian dress in particular.

Macedonian is normally written using the Cyrillic alphabet. *Latinitsa,* or the transliteration of Cyrillic into the Roman alphabet is a slightly complicated process since several Cyrillic letters and the sounds they represent do not correspond one to one with Roman letters. The official system of transliteration involves diacritics over several letters to represent the sounds needed. The editor has decided to spell Macedonian words phonetically, hopefully easing the reader's progress and understanding of the texts. The editor has attempted to standardize the system of spelling as well. The reader will notice there are variations of spelling for names of garments. These are not typos. Names of garments, stitches, materials, and motifs were not the same from region to region or even village to village. The authors have used local spellings and terms when talking about a particular place, thus the word *chikme* is used to mean a type of needle lace in one area and drawn thread embroidery in another area. There is a glossary of terms in the back of the book. The pronunciation of some Macedonian words is unfamiliar to English speakers. The letter "e" at the end of a word is pronounced like the letter "a," chikme sounds like chick-may. The plural is formed by changing the final vowel to i, e. g. darpna to darpni. Stress is on the third syllable from the end, chorabi would be chore'-ah-bee. There are too many examples to explain here.

Skopska Blatiya

Techniques and Materials of Production

JASEMIN NAZIM

SANJA DIMOVSKA

TATJANA GJOGJIOVSKA

SLAVICA HRISTOVA

THE DRESS OF RURAL DWELLERS in Macedonia was the product of a self sufficient domestic economy which depended on the familiar and available textile fibers such as wool, hemp, flax, cotton, silk, and goat hair, as well as on the use of traditional processing methods and technologies. Until the middle of the twentieth century, clothing was mostly manufactured using homemade fabrics. Thenceforth, due to intensive industrialization, traditional dress gradually fell into disuse, while in areas where it remained in use longer, machine-made materials were substituted for hand woven cloth. The manufacture of shepherds' garments made of twill weave woolen fabric persisted longest because they were irreplaceable in the harsh mountain conditions. In addition, people continued to knit some parts of the garment, even though they often bought machine-made yarn. Today, the home manufacture of materials used for clothing is an already forgotten practice.

Extensive agriculture and farming required a lot of manual labor. Consequently, people lived in large family communities which sometimes exceeded sixty members. They were organized in a strict age-related hierarchy. The processing of textile fibers, as well as weaving, tailoring, sewing, embroidering, and knitting were women's responsibilities. The oldest housewife organized and guided the work of all female members in the family. She sorted the fibers for further processing and divided them into portions for each family. According to age and status — child, maiden, betrothed, bride, mother — as well as level of skill, each woman performed her own part of the work related to the manufacture of clothing for herself and other family members.[1]

Mastering of Skills

The incorporation of children into everyday household chores represented an important educational and socializing function of the family. It was mostly the

---

[1] Konstantinov, M., *Opstestven i semeen zivot: Etnologija na Makedoncite* (Social and Family Life: Ethnology of the Macedonians), Macedonian Academy of Sciences and Arts, Skopje, 1996, 199–201.

mother or another older woman in the family who gradually introduced female children into all the stages of clothing manufacture. A needle and thread, spindle, piece of cloth, and a shuttle were put into the cradles of newborn girls in order to arouse diligence and interest in female work. Beginning at five or six years of age, small girls started with the most basic duties, such as hand carding wool. Then they acquired the spinning skill; learning the art of embroidery was considered a kind of elementary education, like learning the alphabet. The mastery of this skill was a confirmation of the girl's maturity, skillfulness, and readiness to assume her responsibilities as a future housewife.

In most cases, the learning process took place among groups of young girls of different ages, starting at seven or eight years old. The girls were gathered together in specially constructed huts where, from the first week of November (St. Dimitar's Day, celebrated on 8 November) until the start of Lent (St. Todor's Day, the first Saturday after the beginning of Lent), from early morning until sunset, they were introduced into the secrets of embroidery by a more experienced and skillful embroiderer. The process lasted around three years. During this time, the young girls were expected to master all embroidery techniques and decorations. They started with small embroidery patterns and the first embroidered chemise was called *uchenichka*, student's chemise. Gradually, they learned more complex embroideries. The final result of the learning process was the bridal chemise. During this period the girls also learned how to knit and make bead jewelry. This kind of learning method, characterized by distinct gender segregation, was a particular form of initiation through which the girls were introduced to the social spheres of life. Separated from the rest of the society in the huts, they entered the world of adult women through the acquisition of basic female skills. Weaving was mastered last, and in this process the more complex weaving techniques were also gradually learned, the hardest being tapestry weaving and the creation of more elaborate motifs. Warping and threading of the loom was executed by older, more experienced weavers.

The acquisition of these skills was important, because it was customary for the maiden to prepare her dowry before marriage i.e. the bridal ensemble and the clothing she would wear until the end of her life. Furthermore, she was also expected to prepare wedding gifts for the family and in-laws, mostly chemises, socks, and towels that had a significant role in the wedding ritual. However, this did not represent the end of female handiwork. Throughout her life, the woman would be responsible for providing her family with clothing.[2]

Growing and Processing of Textile Fibers

The mixed mountain-plain topography and moderate continental and Mediterranean climate in Macedonia provides favorable conditions for raising sheep and goats on pastures and silkworms on mulberry plantations, as well as for planting flax

---

[2] For more details on customs and beliefs while learning the skills, see: Anastasovska, F., *Veruvanjata na Makedoncite povrzani so tekstilnoto tvorestvo:* Makedonski Folklor (*Beliefs of the Macedonians Related to Textile Art:* Macedonian Folklore), 56–57, Folklore Institute "Marko Cepenkov", Skopje, 2001, 509–521; Zdravev, G., *Makedonski narodni nosii 1* (*Macedonian Traditional Dresses 1*), Matica Makedonska, Skopje, 1996, 174–178; Antonova Popstefanieva, M., *Za nekoi folklorni projavi vo vrska so makedonskoto narodno vezenje* (*On Some Folklore Phenomena in Relation to the Macedonian Folk Embroidery*), Works from the Congress of Yugoslav Folklorists in Varazdin, 1957, Zagreb, 1959, 325–326.

and hemp in older times, and more recently, cotton. All the family members were included in the production of fiber. Men were more involved in the rearing and shearing of sheep and goats, as well as preparing the land for sowing, while women played the main role in growing flax and hemp, and in the raising of silkworms.

In order to produce the woven or knitted fabric necessary for the manufacture of garments, fibers had to be sorted, cleaned, and prepared, then spun into yarn for weaving and knitting, or thread for sewing and embroidery. Each fiber – wool, goat hair, silk, hemp, flax, and cotton – required specific tools and technology. The simple wooden tools were manufactured by men or village carpenters. All Slavic people applied the same or similar terms for the textile fibers, processing tools, fiber processing products, work processes, and the way of counting threads while warping, which points to traditions preserved from the Proto-Slavic communities, undoubtedly enriched in Macedonia with experiences from the neighboring non-Slavic Balkan people.

Wool was obtained by shearing sheep. After shearing, the wool was washed and dried, and then combed and carded with hand cards – two wooden brushes with metal bristles. Carding of longer, higher-quality wool required using large-bristle brushes, whereas carding of short hair wool demanded small-bristle brushes. After the mid-twentieth century, wool was taken to the cities to be machine carded. Goat hair obtained from the shearing of goats was not carded; rather it was often mixed with wool, then beaten and fluffed with wooden sticks.

Silk threads were obtained from the silkworm *Bombyx mori*. The silkworm larvae fed on mulberry leaves, molting several times before spinning cocoons in which they pupate. The cocoons were then scalded with hot water and the threads were unwound using tiny twigs, after which they were twisted.

Flax and hemp were planted in fields suitable for them to thrive. After the harvest, they were dried in sheaves and then soaked in rivers or ponds to make them soft, which was followed by another drying session. The fibers were then separated from the woody part of the stems by beating them with a wooden tool, known as a break. Eventually, the shredder waste was cleaned with a boar-bristle brush and the fibers were carded.

Cotton was dried after the harvest and the seeds were removed by hand or with a wooden cotton gin, after which it was fluffed using a wooden bow made from a small stick and string. In more recent times, people bought machine-spun cotton thread. [3]

Spinning, Reeling, and Warping

After the carding process, the fluffed and straightened fibers were arranged in long rolls called slivers that were then spun into weaving yarn. Generally, the sliver was tied onto a wooden distaff that a woman tucked into the left side of her sash. Distaffs differed according to the shape of the top, i.e. the head where the sliver is

---

[3]   For growing and processing of textile fibers see: Krstevska, M., *Narodno tkaenje* (*Traditional Weaving*), Social and Spiritual Aspects of Material Culture, University "Ss. Cyril and Methodius" – Skopje, Faculty of Natural Sciences and Mathematics, Institute of Ethnology and Anthropology, Skopje, 2009, 350–360; Radaus-Ribaric, J., *O tekstilnom rukotvorstvu na tlu Jugoslavije kroz vekove:* Carolija niti (*On Hand-Made Textiles in Yugoslavia through Ages:* The Wonder of Weaving), MGC, Zagreb, 1988, 13–24.

attached, which can be forked, spade, round, or tubby shaped. Special types of distaffs were used for the spinning of wool, hemp, flax, or cotton. This manner of spinning enabled the woman to move freely, so she could simultaneously perform other household chores.

When spinning, the fibers were pulled from the sliver with the left hand, while the right hand rotated the spindle, which dangled loosely downwards as the twisted fibers wound themselves around it. The spindle was a rounded wooden stick, thicker towards the middle and pointed at the ends. Before the spinning process started, a spindle whorl made of wood, clay or stone, which controlled the movement of the spindle with its weight, was placed at the bottom part of the spindle. The spindle was rotated clockwise when the spinning was done for the purpose of weaving, making finer tightly spun yarn for the warp, but thicker and softer for the weft. Counterclockwise spinning was performed for knitting socks. Spinning was also done without a distaff, especially for obtaining weft yarn. The sliver was placed on the ground and the yarn was pulled with the left hand, while the right rotated the spindle upwards. After the beginning of the twentieth century, the spinning wheel began to be used for spinning as well.

The yarn was wound into a skein on a stick. The number of turns around the stick served as a measure for the warp's length. The basic measuring unit was three turns. The yarns wound around the stick were scalded with boiling water to set the twist. After drying, the yarn from the stick was placed on a skein holder and rolled into balls. If a thicker yarn was needed, the yarn was plied with a spindle.

It was only the woolen embroidery threads that were prepared in a special archaic manner: they were twisted only by hand from the highest-quality wool which, unlike other skeins of yarn, was dyed before twisting. Each thread was twisted separately to obtain the necessary length. Two women worked together–one pulled the wool off the sliver and passed it on to the other who twisted it between her palms.

Warping was usually performed on wooden pegs stuck in the ground. Warp threads, which had been rolled into several balls and placed in different household dishes, were carried around the pegs simultaneously with a warping paddle with multiple holes through which the yarns were threaded. The last two pegs were placed next to each other and the threads were crossed around them forming the shed. The warped yarn was then taken off the pegs, braided into a warp chain, and then wound on the warp beam of the loom.[4]

Weaving

After preparing the warp and weft yarn the weaving process could begin. Weaving was performed on a two or four harness horizontal treadle loom. The most frequently used technique in Macedonia was balanced plain weave, equal on both the front and back side. The hemp, flax, and cotton cloth, as well as some of the woolen

4   Spinning, reeling and warping are elaborately described in: Krstevska, M., *Kolekcijata na furki od Muzejot na Makedonija: Zbornik Etnologija 2* (*Distaff Collection of the Museum of Macedonia:* Collection of Ethnology 2), Museum of Macedonia, Skopje, 2002, 35–51; Krstevska, M., *Narodno tkaenje* (*Traditional Weaving*), 350–360; Krsteva, A., *Domasnoto tekstilno proizvodstvo–Strezevo* (*Domestic Textile Manufacture–Strezhevo*), Manuscript in print.

clothing materials, were plain-woven with one pair of harnesses and treadles on the loom. Woolen fabrics which were usually fulled, and part of the linen and cotton cloth used for upper garments, were twill-woven in a basic diagonal weave using four harnesses and treadles. The twill-weave woolen fabric was commonly finished in fulling mills with a water-driven mechanism moving large wooden hammers that beat the woven fabrics scalded in boiling water. The fulling process produced a thick, firm, and nappy woven material, which was a good insulator against cold and humidity.

Given that women were traditionally the only weavers in Macedonia, weaving never developed into a professional craft organized into guilds like other male crafts. Each woman wove everything needed for the family by herself. However, there were poorer women who did custom weaving of linen or woolen cloth, whether for their fellow villagers or for sale at markets and fairs; places where potential customers or middlemen appeared as well.[5]

Dyeing and Bleaching

Flax, hemp, and cotton were not dyed. Woven cloth was bleached by soaking it in tubs full of water and cow dung, after which it was washed in the river and spread out on the grass to dry in the sun. The finished fabrics were twisted into rolls and kept that way until they were to be made into clothing. The multicolored cotton cloth used for upper garments was made with machine-spun and dyed thread.

Twill-weave woolen garments were mostly manufactured by using undyed wool in its natural shades—white, gray, black, and brown. Some of the twill-weave woolen fabrics were dyed after the process of fulling. Aprons, sashes, and certain types of upper woolen garments were woven using previously dyed multicolored wool. Until the emergence of aniline dyes at the beginning of the twentieth century, wool yarn was dyed exclusively with natural dyes of plant origin. It was dyed at home by women or taken to artisan dyers in the cities who used old recipes which involved soaking and boiling parts of plants. Red was the most popular color for embroidery and it was obtained from the root of the madder plant *Rubia tinctorum*.

Materials for Manufacture of Garments

Male and female garments, including chemises, under-chemises, dickeys, trousers and pleated apron-skirts, head pieces, and decorative towels were all manufactured using homemade plain-woven white cloth made of hemp, flax, and cotton. Linen and cotton cloth was produced in different thicknesses, densities, and widths according to how they were to be used. The commonly woven fabrics were long and narrow due to the width of the loom. Older chemises were made of hemp or flax, whereas after the beginning of the twentieth century, the predominant cloth was cotton. In addition to cloth of a single fiber, union cloth made of hemp or flax warp and cotton weft, was also woven.

5   Information about weaving techniques and dry fulling mills is found in: Krstevska, M., *Narodno tkaenje (Traditional Weaving)*, 350–360; Nedelkovski, B., *Valavicarstvoto vo Makedonija so osvrt na suvite valavici vo s. Virovo–Zeleznik: Zbornik Etnologija 2 (Fulling in Macedonia with Reference to the Dry Fuller Mills in Virovo Village–Zeleznik: Collection of Ethnology 2)*, Museum of Macedonia, Skopje, 2002, 113–12.

Although cotton clothing became more common, certain more archaic parts of the costume, such as bridal head pieces, were still made from hemp and flax cloth. These materials were also used to line certain parts of the costume, but they too were later substituted with cotton cloth. Untailored pieces of hemp cloth were used for wrapping around the woman's body in order to obtain a plumper appearance and to make the chemise worn over them stand straighter.

In addition to ordinary white cloth, plain-weave cotton cloth with vertical warp stripes was also made. The stripes were obtained by warping thicker spun or dyed cotton or silk yarn. Generally, the stripes were symmetrically arranged on the edges or they repeated following a certain pattern across the entire width of the fabric. This cloth was used for the manufacture of both male and female garments, including chemises, trousers, and decorative towels. The thicker twill-weave cotton cloth was used for the manufacture of sleeveless upper garments, while in the cold mountain areas it also served for making men's shirts and trousers. Pure silk cloth or cotton cloth striped with silk was used for making head pieces and decorative towels.

Wool yarn in its natural colors like white or gray-brown, or dyed black, red, brown, and blue was essential for outer garments traditionally worn in Macedonia. This type of woolen fabric could be a lighter plain-weave or the heavier twill-weave. Fulled twills were used for the manufacture of male garments and female garments worn over the chemise. Garments of different lengths and cuts were worn on the upper body and could be with or without sleeves, collars, and hoods. On the lower body, men wore different types of breeches, as well as various kinds of gaiters worn over the knitted socks. (See page 132) The hems of linen garments adorned with rich embroidery on the front side were lined with twill-weave woolen fabric. Un-fulled twill-weave woolen fabric was only used for certain specific parts of the garment. Shepherds' cloaks were made from an impervious, twill-woven, fulled, and very thick fabric made from a mixture of wool and goat hair.

Patterned plain-weave fabric was made from finer wool yarn. It could be striped or finely checkered. The background was mostly red, black, and blue with varicolored or discrete monochromatic vertical stripes. It was used for the manufacture of male and female upper garments of different cuts and lengths. Garments made of these fabrics were commonly lined with cotton cloth, quilted, and hand-darned and are of more recent origin than the twill woven ones. They show the influence of Ottoman styles. (See page 244)

Special techniques were applied in weaving woolen aprons, sashes, and garters. Aprons, usually composed of two pieces, were plain-woven and ornamented with straight stripes or checks, which was performed by shooting a multicolored weft with the shuttle. Aprons having more elaborate geometrical ornaments, mostly diamonds, were made in tapestry weave identical to that of kilims. The ornaments of certain aprons were performed by using pick-up sticks. Sashes could be plain-woven or twill-woven. Narrower sashes were woven using four heddles, but without reeding the warp. The pattern was determined by a particular arrangement of the colors of the warp threads, as well as by their threading and treadling order. The monochromatic weft was shot with the shuttle and firmly packed with a stick. The warp yarns formed the ornaments composed of narrow stripes and small geometrical motifs. Supporting straps or garters worn to hold up the socks were woven by using a hole-and-slot loom. In certain areas, even some parts of the head pieces or chemises were decorated with woven appliqués. Men's hats were made from wool by specialized artisans using the felting technique which didn't involve any weaving.

Traditional dress was also made with materials that were not homemade. Machine-woven white cotton cloth, used for sewing chemises and head pieces, decorative scarves and towels, turbans, dickeys, and more recently aprons, was purchased in the cities or brought by migrant workers from abroad. Certain upper garments were made using cotton cloth with blue and white stripes. Patterned or monochromatic cotton material, mostly red, was used in the manufacture of under-chemises and some outerwear of a more recent type or cut. This type of cloth was also used for lining the chemise sleeves, collar, and chest opening and for hemming the woolen garments and aprons. Silk and mixed silk monochromatic or patterned materials were purchased for the manufacture of scarves and decorative towels, aprons, half-sleeves, dickeys, and dresses. Colored woolen cloth and velvet were used for making upper garments with or without sleeves, which were mostly decorated with silver-gilt embroidery and cords, as well as for dickeys and half-sleeves. Since these materials were costly, they were mainly used for decoration.[6]

Knitwear

Only certain parts of the costumes were knitted. Commonly knitted items were socks and half-socks which covered the legs from the ankle to the calves, half-sleeves for covering the arms from the palms to the elbows, as well as undershirts, hats, and gloves. Wool was spun specifically for this purpose. Prior to knitting, the yarn was dyed in different colors. Apart from wool, knitters also used cotton and silk yarn, as well as silver-gilt thread. Knitting of socks started at the toe; they were knitted from the reverse side and each new row used previously measured threads. The heel part was knitted with two needles, whereas the remaining section of the socks were done using three or five.

Most strikingly ornamented are those parts of the socks that are most visible – the top of the foot and surrounding ankle area. Male and female socks and half-socks made until the first decades of the twentieth century used multi-colored wool and were knitted in horizontal friezes with various motifs, squares with motifs in their central part, or only with larger central motifs. Geometrical motifs were predominant and, together with the coloring, they were in harmony with the decoration on the rest of the outfit. In certain areas white cotton thread was embroidered over the knitted motif and bead and sequin decorations were added. The bottom of the foot, namely the heel and toes, were differently, but not less, decorated. The top of the socks were tied with twisted or plaited woolen strings. To make dressing easier, certain types of half-socks had slits on the sides that were hemmed with decorative cords and loops used for threading the sock ties. Narrow woven garters were tied over them as well.

---

[6]   Materials used for manufacture of garments are described in: Zdravev, *Makedonski narodni nosii 1* (*Macedonian Traditional Dresses 1*)

Socks were among the first elements of dress to change with time. After the beginning of the twentieth century their decoration was simplified, thus only monochromatic or striped socks were knitted. The knitting of half-sleeves was gradually abandoned and replaced with sewn fabric construction.

Simple plaiting techniques were used for making multicolored woolen ties for aprons, socks, breeches, and linen trousers. Child's swaddling clothes were bound with a long cord of plaited woolen threads. Long black woolen and goat hair sashes for girdling around the waist, as well as heavy black woolen hair extensions were also made by plaiting. [7]

Leather and Fur

Some outer garments were made from leather and fur. Leather was processed by specialized craftsmen grouped in several cities in Macedonia. The hides were tanned by the tanners and then sold to various artisans for further manufacture. The largest consumers were the makers of *opinci,* a kind of shoe made from one piece of leather, which were worn by the majority of the rural population. The opinci intended for the summer were made from boar skin, whereas waterproof cow skin was used for making winter opinci. They were tied with hemp strings. Villagers themselves made opinci from untanned hides. Slipper makers manufactured footwear such as slippers and slipper shoes. Most sought-after were the *emenii,* a kind of flat shoe made of goatskin. After the mid-nineteenth century, slipper making was replaced by the shoe making craft under the influence of European fashion when villagers started wearing shoes made of *saftiyan,* goatskin, especially for formal occasions. Various models of shoes were manufactured depending on the fashion.

The *kozhuvari* were furriers who only manufactured garments made of sheepskin, which they processed themselves. Male, female, and children's upper garments, namely sheepskin coats with or without sleeves and wool on the inside were cut, sewn, and decorated with varicolored leather appliqués. Only shepherd's sheepskin coats had wool on the outside.

The *kyurchii,* on the other hand, were furriers who trimmed with fur the upper garments previously sewn by tailors. They generally used sheep and lamb pelts, as well as game fur–bear, wolf, fox, and rabbit–which they themselves processed. They also made lambskin hats, mainly black, that were widely worn by men. These two types of furriers manufactured finished products for sale, but they also performed custom manufacturing in which they always considered the local characteristics of the traditional dress. [8]

Sewing and Decoration of Garments

Women used to cut, sew, embroider, and adorn most of the garments for the family members, especially the linen chemises and trousers, scarves, aprons, and some

---

[7]   On the knitwear in Macedonia see: *Zdravev, G., Makedonski narodni nosii 1 (Macedonian Traditional Dresses 1). Krsteva, A., Narodnoto pletivo vo cetiri poloski sela*: Zbornik na Etnoloskiot muzej–Skopje (*Folk Knitwear in Four Polog Villages*: Journal of the Ethnological Museum of Skopje), Ethnological Museum, Skopje, 1965, 83–94.

upper garments. They were of simple standard cut, thus taking into account the economical use of fabrics and the fine finish of seams and hems that also functioned as garment ornaments. The basic decoration of linen garments was the embroidery performed with multi-colored woolen threads. Apart from wool, they also used cotton, silk, and silver-gilt threads.

Artisan Manufacture

Other elements of the costume, especially the outer garments, were made by specialized artisans, tailors and embroiderers. They used fabrics, cuts, and decorations consistent with local custom, taking into account the requirements of each separate micro region. *Abadjii* were tailors who sewed garments from twill or plain-weave fulled woolen fabric. They went to villages upon request and sewed according to the families' needs. The abadjii manufactured mostly male garments for everyday use, such as breeches, short waistcoats and jackets, which they hemmed and decorated with cords.

Terzii were tailors who made feast-day wear from woolen and cotton homemade fabrics. Some parts of the garment were made from ready-made materials. The terzii, as well as the abadjii, worked upon invitation in village households, but they also owned stores in the cities where they sold ready-made garments. They sewed male and female upper garments, various types of jackets, and short waistcoats. The terzii also made cotton waistcoats and quilted jackets padded with cotton.

The terzii were also accompanied by professional tailor-embroiderers *srmadjii* who decorated the garments. They embroidered the garments with silver-gilt thread called *srma,* thin gold, silver, or copper wire twisted around cotton thread. Garments were adorned with cords and braids along the hems. The ornaments were embroidered following outlined motifs on the cloth. The silver-gilt threads were couched onto the outline using a fine thread. Apart from silver-gilt, cheaper cotton and silk threads—*bukme,* were also used for embroidering.[9]

Trims

The entire decoration of the traditional ensemble consisted of cords, ready-made ribbons, and braids made of silk, velvet, and cotton in different colors, all of which served for trimming, as well as embroidery, beads, sequins, coins, fringes, and laces. The most prevalent technique in the decoration of upper garments was the application of pieces of woolen cloth, twill-weave woolen fabric, velvet, and mono-

8   Information about leather and fur processing and manufacturing of garments and shoes can be found in: Klickova, V., *Kurcisko-kozuvarskiot zanaet i esnaf vo Skopje* (*Furrier's Craft and Guild in Skopje*), Ethnological Museum, Skopje, 1959, 28–37; Kovaceva-Kostadinova, V., *Zanayati v yugozapadnite blgarski zemi x v–x i x vek* (*Crafts in the Southwest Bulgarian Countries*), Bulgarian Academy of Sciences, Sofia, 1991, 78–90; Konstantinov, M., *Makedonci,* Narodite na svetot, 6 (*Macedonians: Peoples of the World, 6*), Maring, Skopje 1992, 290.

9   For homemade and artisan manufacture of clothes see: Cepenkov, M., *Makedonski narodni umotvorbi* 10 (*Macedonian Folk Art, 10*), Makedonska Kniga, Skopje, 1972, 27–37; Krsteva, A., *Skopskite srmadjii: Zbornik I* (*Skopje Goldwork Artisans*: Collection 1), Museum of the City of Skopje, Skopje, 1964, 29–36; Licenoska, Z., *Soopstenija od terenot za poslednite srmakesi vo Makedonija,* Zbornik na Etnoloskiot muzej -Skopje (*Reports from the Field Researches on the Last Embroideres with Silver- Gilt Threads*) Bulletin of the Ethnological Museum, Skopje, 1965, 221–230; Zdravev, G., *Makedonski narodni nosii 1* (*Macedonian Traditional Dresses 1*), Matica Makedonska, Skopje, 1996, 21–169.

chromatic or patterned cotton or silk cloth. Appliqué served as decoration even when it was only sewn on the hems of the garment. However, appliqués sewn onto the chest part, back, sleeves, and adjacent hems of the garment, as well as onto head pieces, aprons, sashes, and gaiters, served solely as a base for additional embroidery and trims. A more recent phenomenon in costume decoration was the substitution of the chemise embroidery with applied pieces of woolen cloth, velvet, and monochromatic or patterned cotton cloth.

The trimming and decoration with twisted and plaited cords called *gaitan* appears in almost all outer garments in Macedonia. This involved using homemade or artisan-made woolen, cotton, silk, and silver-gilt cords of different thickness and quality. The dominant color was black, but red, blue, and green were also present. [10]

The most impressive and at the same time most archaic costume decoration are the twisted woolen, silk, and cotton fringes. They were of different color, length, and thickness, and as such, they were sewn onto the sleeves, chest, and back of upper garments, then, onto aprons, head pieces and decorative towels, as well as on the ends of sashes. Bridal head pieces had the largest, longest, and most diverse fringe decorations. Some of them had their woolen or natural hair fringes partially braided and added to the hair. In addition to the fringes, the hems of certain upper garments, aprons, and scarves were also ornamented with multicolored woolen tufts and pompoms. [11]

Various kinds of lace were used for decorating the chemise chest opening, lower hem and sleeves, as well as the hems of aprons, sashes, head pieces, decorative towels, and handkerchiefs. Lace is mostly found on costumes that have no embroidery. The use of lace in costume decoration was adopted from urban areas. Several kinds of lace were made. Needle lace made from multicolored cotton threads with geometrical, floral, and animal motifs was worked with a sewing needle. This tool was also used for performing the special decoration on the seams of chemises in some regions of Western Macedonia. A crochet hook was used for making white lacy trim, whereas a hairpin frame was necessary for creating monochromatic cotton and silk lace to which beads and sequins were added. [12]

Jewelry

Jewelry constitutes an integral part of the costume. The most favorite practice was adornment with flowers which were tucked behind the ear, into the sash and hair, or carried in the hand. Bridal head wreaths were made from basil, box tree branches, and ivy. Maidens and brides also adorned themselves with dyed goose or peacock feathers. Jewelry composed of smaller and larger glass beads started to be made after the beginning of the twentieth century. This material was used for making female necklaces, bracelets, and belts. Male watch-chains with geometrical and floral ornaments were worn on the chest and sash, or they were used for leading the dance. This type of jewelry was made by girls and young wives.

---

10   Zdravev, G., *Makedonski narodni nosii 1* (*Macedonian Traditional Dresses 1*).

11   Ibid.

12   Ibid.; Zdravev, G., *Narodnite tanteli sorki vo Ovcepolieto* (*Folk Laces–Sorki in the Ovce Pole Region*), Folklore Institute, Library of the Journal "Makedonski folklor", 5, Skopje, 1975.

Jewelry was made by urban silversmiths from silver, gold, copper, and various alloys by applying techniques such as casting, embossing, engraving, filigree, and granulation. Some parts of the jewelry had coral, enamel, dyed glass, and mother-of-pearl added. The kinds of pieces they created were similar, but they were still made to fit local criteria. Female jewelry was numerous and diverse. Among the pieces of jewelry used as adornment were the decorative pins for the head and chest, buttons, silver and coin caps, earrings, necklaces, rings, bracelets, belts, and buckles. A particularly favorite piece was the silver, gold, and brass coins, which were in some parts substituted with *tontuzi*–imitation coins made from brass and tin. The coins were worn strung around the neck, chest, or sash, but they were also attached to the hats, rings, and earrings. They were densely sewn on a piece of fabric which was worn on the chest and called *gyerdan*.

Men wore silver watch-chains attached to the chest. Weapons manufactured by gunsmiths and decorated with silver and mother-of-pearl by silversmiths and mother-of-pearl artisans were a component of men's adornment. [13]

Beliefs and Customs

In the traditional and patriarchal life of the village community, everything was imbued with strictly determined rules and customs, based on centuries of rooted traditions, many of which are of pre-Christian origin. The whole system of ritual practice and beliefs aimed to ensure successful work, health, and fertility to humans, crops, and cattle and their protection from natural disasters, vermin, evil eyes, evil forces, and spells. There were numerous bans and recommendations for work or starting work, related to certain parts of the day, week, or whole periods during the year, usually associated with calendar holidays. The phases of the moon and women's menstrual cycles also played an important role in the timing of tasks.

Certain actions were practiced to ensure the successful performance of each stage of textile work, from spinning to embroidery. For a good start of the spinning process, women began to spin near running water with the belief that evil would flow away with the water. The first spun thread was thrown into the fire, while the initial spinning threads were thrown on the roof to be blown off by the wind. To retain the color of the yarn, the woman who dyed it was not supposed to utter a sound. The warped yarn ready for weaving was put on a high place–tree or door–for the work to grow, over the bread chest for the loom to be full and not waste a lot of weft, and it was also hung on an iron object for the woven cloth to be firm.

It was believed that the places where warp was wound were haunted by demon creatures or souls of the dead. Therefore, they poured water and inscribed crosses at these sites, and they also let an animal pass through them first. It was not allowed to step over the yarn. The woman who warped the loom was supposed to talk a lot to make the loom shed open wide. Before weaving started the loom was adorned with flowers so that process of weaving would be joyful and would flourish. They kicked a bowl of water under the loom to make the work flow like water. They also inscribed crosses to keep the devil from coming at night and weaving on the loom.

---

[13] Delinikolova, Z., *Narodniot nakit i kitenjeto vo Makedonija (Folk Jewelry and Ornamentation in Macedonia)*, Ethnological Museum of Macedonia, Skopje, 1982.

The magical power of the yarn was used to bring health to people and fertility to crops and cattle, as well as to make women's delivery easier. In order to make children healthy, yarn was wound on a piece of bread or a walnut and given to the children to eat. To make fruit set on the fruit trees, they tied scraps of warp yarn to the trees and to the hands of people who planted watermelons. These threads were also given to the poor so that they would have a good harvest. [14]

Protective and Magical Function of Garments

In Macedonian customs and beliefs the dominant role was played by relics of pagan beliefs. These were practiced along with the Christian Orthodox religion. In order to illustrate this, we will introduce several examples from the isolated mountain area of Mariovo, where numerous archaic elements were preserved, both in the appearance of and the beliefs related to the protective and magical function of traditional dress. [15]

The ensemble of elements, or only its individual parts, had the power to protect people from supernatural forces, diseases and death, as well as evil and envious eyes. People are most vulnerable in the three critical periods of their life – birth, marriage, and death. Therefore immediately after birth a baby was wrapped in a new woolen apron from the mother. The pattern of black and white stripes on the apron and swaddling clothes symbolized strength and resistance. A bundle of red woolen fringes, basil, and a metal coin were attached to the baby's head to protect it from evil eyes. Each of these elements was symbolic on its own but as a whole, like every other decoration, they functioned to draw the attention of evil spirits and any envious or evil eyes of the people back to themselves and away from the newborn. Old women were considered to be the most dangerous, as it was believed that they sucked the life force out of young people through their eyes.

Spirits and ghosts from the Underworld, especially the vampire, were considered to be most dangerous for the newlyweds during the wedding ceremony. People's evil eyes were presumed dangerous too. It was believed that they could deprive the bride and groom of their sexual force along with their ability to conceive and create new life. One of the main functions of the wedding costume and jewelry was to protect the newlyweds throughout the entire wedding ceremony until the wedding night. The appearance of the bride and groom was changed so that they wouldn't be recognized by apparitions, and their faces were covered with pieces of garments. Evil eyes were drawn and retained on the numerous and gaudy jewelry.

When someone passed away, everyone in the household wore their oldest ripped clothes. Jackets were worn inside out. The garments worn were expected to be in darker colors. Women unbraided their hair and tied black scarves on their heads, whereas men wore black hats and stopped shaving and cutting their hair. Jewelry

---

[14]   Anastasovska, F., *Veruvanjata na Makedoncite povrzani so tekstilnoto tvorestvo*: Makedonski Folklor (*Beliefs of the Macedonians related to Textile Art*: Macedonian Folklore) 56–57, Folklore Institute "Marko Cepenkov", Skopje, 2001, 509–521.

[15]   Very archaic beliefs on the protective and magic function of the dress were researched in the mountanious region of Mariovo in the 1930' by: Radovanovic, V., *Narodna Nosnja u Marijovu*: Glasnik Skopskog naucnog drustva, knj. xiv (*Traditional Dress in Mariovo*: Journal of the Skopje Scientific Society, book xiv), Social Sciences Department 8, Skopje, 1935, 21–46.

was not worn on such occasions. They did all this in order to protect themselves from the evil spirits who brought death, as well as from the soul of the deceased, which lingered around the hearth for some time after death. The living believed that, being disguised in this way, they wouldn't be recognized. During the period from the fortieth day until a year after death, the elements of this protective disguise were gradually abandoned.

Certain parts of the costume, especially the jewelry and other decorations, had a protective effect particularly during youth. Since female jewelry was known to offer the most efficient protection, it was sometimes worn by young men. Special importance was attached to both the silver cross and triangular Muslim amulet which protected from fairies that could cause death.

Certain motifs of a protective function can be found in the costume's decoration, especially the embroidery. Such motifs were the cross and the rooster, a single or double hook-shaped motif more powerful than the cross. The rooster that crowed at the break of dawn chased away the devil, vampires, and apparitions. The stylized dog paw represented the dog as chief protector of man and home from apparitions. The triangle was also considered protective and frequently appeared as an amulet. Ornaments had magical functions as well as protective ability. Snake and lion motifs contributed to better health, while chicks, roots, and grapes assured fertility to those wearing them. The dominant red color of the embroidery had the same magical function.

The entire ensemble, together with its smallest integral parts, was the very embodiment and sign of the individual who wore it, thus it was used as an intermediary for certain magical practices such as curing by magic and sorcery. Applying these magical activities to the garments of the imperiled person contributed to removing the evil brought about by supernatural forces or creatures. As well as white magic, garments were also used for performing black magic. People who served the devil could harm, bring evil, or cause death to other people through their clothing. It was also believed that donating parts of the clothing of a sick person to the church, such as a chemise, an apron, socks, or a hat, would bring health or cause recovery.

Similar beliefs stressing the importance of a person's clothing existed all over Macedonia. A person's dress functioned not only as protection from the elements and a means of beautification but also as an active element, indicating the individual's social status and group belonging. At the same time it served as a representative or intermediary for humans communicating with both the real and supernatural world.

Kolo Dance, Skopska Blatiya

The Embroidery on Macedonian Traditional Dress

ANGELINA KRSTEVA

EMBROIDERY REPRESENTS an important aspect of the treasury of traditional Macedonian cultural values. It was formerly an essential part of Macedonian traditional dress, having its own functions and meaning within the social, and in particular, rural environments. People in each region used color, motifs, stitches, and placement of embroidery to distinguish their dress from neighboring communities. Aesthetic norms and local standards developed and were passed down through the generations to create recognizable village or regional styles that served as markers of identity.

Skill in needlework was expected of all the female members of a family. Accordingly, great emphasis was placed on teaching and learning these skills beginning in childhood. Young girls received group instruction from older, more skilled girls for a period of three years. Students assisted with embroidery of the teacher's trousseau in exchange for instruction.

Embroidery was mostly used to decorate women's dress, especially the chemise, known as *koshula*. Usually calf or ankle length with long, full sleeves, the white dress-like chemise was made from home produced cotton, linen, or hemp cloth. Lavish embroidery also decorated the various forms of women's head coverings, *sokay, ubrusi, marami, darpni,* and *korpi.* Embroidery was also present on some outer garments made of cotton cloth, *sai,* as well as in those made of thick woolen fabric, *klashenici, shayaci,* and *gornici.* The chemises and outer garments made of cotton were embroidered on directly, while for the heavier wool clothing the stitch work was first done on red cotton cloth and then sewn in place.

The finest quality wool was chosen for embroidery yarn. Typically, it was prepared at home where it was twisted repeatedly by hand without the use of any tools. Two girls worked together. One girl held the fleece and drew out the fibers while the other girl rolled it between her palms to spin it. She then plied the yarn by doubling and twisting it back on itself. The yarn was prepared in short lengths, just enough to work with in the needle. Less frequently, a spindle and distaff were used to spin the wool. Wool yarn was dyed at home or by professional dyers using plant materials that ensured stable colors. The availability of aniline dyes at the end of the nineteenth century significantly altered the traditional color palette.

Silk was also used on special occasion and ceremonial garments. Silk threads were often purchased, but in some places silk worms were raised for this purpose. Some-

1) Detail of page 178

times, women also used purchased metallic thread called *srma,* in either silver or gold, on bridal garments.

Hand woven cloth with a finer warp and a thicker weft made a suitable foundation for counted thread embroidery, one of the main types of Macedonian embroidery. Embroidery was most often worked from the back of the fabric with multiple techniques. Some stitches such as relief or raised, hem, and drawn thread stitches were worked from the front. Each new length of thread was skillfully spliced to the end of the previous one so the join was invisible and there were no knots.

The most frequently used stitch in Macedonian embroidery was *polnez,* oblique or slanted Slav stitch, which had several variations and was worked slanting either to the left or the right. The motifs were first outlined with fine black thread using a stitch called *lozeno, crneto,* or *orano,* double running or Holbein stitch. This sketch might remain partially visible but was frequently completely covered by the slanted filling stitches worked in heavier, colored threads. Several variations of outline stitch, called *travchi, tegli,* or *sindyati,* were used to delineate sections of the design. Raised stitches, *skorchi, nofteno,* and others, made by using tightly or loosely twisted woolen threads, were only used in certain embroidery designs, as were the drawn thread techniques *kinatica* and *kyesme.* Cross stitch, *krvchinya,* was mostly used as an accent and only in isolated cases as a main technique. Vertical straight stitch, *podlachno,* appeared in several versions. It was also known as *sokaechko,* because it was typically used on a type of head piece called *sokay.* The edges of the embroidered areas were always finished with various kinds of overcast, hem stitches, or other needle techniques, *odmetnato, opshieno,* and *poplit.*

Red and black are the dominant colors of Macedonian embroidery. Accents of blue, green, yellow and more rarely white are seen in more recent work. Sometimes two shades of red were used in the same embroidery, a brilliant vermillion called *alova* or *alska* and a dark red called *gyuvezna* or *chista.* These two shades were substituted for the older variant, a sober dark red color – *brozdena,* that was originally derived from the roots of the madder plant. With the penetration of aniline colors, the vermilion color became orange in many embroidery designs, whereas the dark red became even darker. Only in certain Macedonian embroidery designs in the older samples, a third and darkest shade of red is concurrently present.

Macedonian embroidery is characterized by its strictly geometrical expression. Geometrical abstraction "enslaves" even the rare use of floral and figurative motifs. Despite the fact that the names of many motifs are related to real world concepts, their interpretation usually renders them unrecognizable. The motifs often refer back to ancient symbols, renderings, and cultural traditions. The practice of creating the outline of a pattern on a chemise in a less visible place or on a separate piece of cloth contributed to the continued use of many ornamental motifs. These visual references or samplers were known as *zaorok, zalozok,* and *zavez.* (1)

Rural women's dress in Macedonia was extremely varied and highly localized; it was produced and worn into the middle of the twentieth century in some parts of the country. Embroidery styles were associated with specific geographic locations and functioned to identify the wearer. Dress changed over time; the embroidery applied to garments changed as well. In fact, embroidery was not only a required skill but was also the foremost activity where an individual woman's creative talents were strongly expressed. Thus it was more dynamic and changed a little more rapidly than other elements of dress.

Women's dress in each village or group of villages in western Macedonia showed distinct embroidery. This is most evident in the Brsyak ethnographic entity, where an amazing multitude of different local types and variations flourished. On the other hand, certain similarities in the embroidery design were common to several ethnographic entities. For instance, the white-on-white embroidery at the bottom of the chemise appears in several areas: the Miyak-Debar and in some parts of the Brsyak and South-Macedonian entities. Both the specific and shared characteristics of dress are mutually intricately intertwined, particularly west of the Vardar River. This is mostly due to the geographical parceling, the dislocation of the population, as well as the different cultural influences in this part of Macedonia. However, it is important to understand that even with the external influences, the mutual intertwining, as well as innovations in the use of embroidery, still adhered to the basic traditional local standards. Hence ideas and techniques were shared, accepted, and maintained further as a general distinction of each separate group.

An interesting example of adhering to centuries old traditions is the dress and its embroidery decoration of the Miyak group, known for the maintenance of their ethnic identity and resistance to foreign influences. Miyaks originally lived in the district of Mala Reka in western Macedonia. In the beginning of the eighteenth century they began to migrate to the east-southeast and established the villages of Ehloetc in the Kicheviya district, Smilevo in the Zheleznik district, Oreshe and Papradishte in the Azot district near Tito Veles, and also settled in the city of Krushevo. Until recently the Miyaks all maintained the basic features of their dress virtually unchanged. Composition, placement, techniques, and color preferences, along with terminology have been preserved as well.

The similarity that is evident today in the dress of these geographically dispersed groups indicates that their forms and decoration were fully developed by the time migration began in the eighteenth century. Nevertheless, it is understandable that in each location over time subtle changes and distinctions occurred so that the dress of each of these Miyak groups diverged slightly and became recognizable. Some differences in terminology appeared as well.

Embroidery is most evident on the female chemise and the head scarf called *darpna*. Miyak women typically spun their embroidery yarn using a distaff and spindle. The wool yarns were then dyed in shades of red and used to decorate the sleeves and either side of the front opening of the typical chemise. White, green, and yellow cotton or silk threads were used as accents, as well as metallic threads for special occasions. Black appeared very rarely. The hem of the skirt was finished with white stitching.

The sleeves of the chemise best represent the Miyak style of embroidery. The layout of horizontal and vertical bands extending all the way to the shoulder is unique in Macedonia but common to all Miyak groups. The drawn thread technique, kinatica, gives the sleeve its distinct appearance. It is worked by removing selected warp or weft yarns and then tightly wrapping the remaining yarns in a specific order using needle and thread to create both the color patterns and the characteristic spaces. Horizontal and vertical bands of kinatica of varying width

characteristic spaces. Horizontal and vertical bands of kinatica of varying width are separated by rows of outline stitch, sindjati. (2) At the top and bottom of the sleeve there are areas of oblique Slav stitch, in the Miyak dialect called *p'lnatica,* containing small rectangular shapes. The same stitches are used on a small piece of cloth that is then sewn on to the chest area. The bottom of the chemise is stitched with white thread and the garment sections are joined with needle lace called *chikme.* Chikme was usually done by the more experienced needlewomen using a sewing needle. (3)

The distinctions in the embroidery on the chemise of the different Miyak groups are visible in certain details and variations, as well as, to a certain degree, in the terminology. In the original Miyak group in Mala Reka, the embroidery on the sleeves of the chemise is distinguished by use of dark red with green and yellow accents and an abundance of white. In some Mala Reka villages, the embroidery design consists of one more color, the darkest red—*temno chista,* which is not used among other Miyak groups except those in the neighboring villages of Dolna Reka. The sleeve is composed of five to seven drawn work bands. Generally, the drawn-work designs here are the most elaborated in width and ornament. The narrowest band was called *tegel,* the wider one *trekyache,* and the widest *kyesme,* which was usually in the middle. There was another band called *moshkare* which was most frequently present above the last horizontal hemstitch band and was considered to be the most colorful. Generally, and as a rule, this band was supposed to distinguish itself from the others.

The wedding chemise called *tnoka* is set apart from the others by specific finishing embroidery above the horizontal and between the vertical bands. This embroidery, called *pisani podvevci,* was built into a pyramidal shape using the *pisanechko,* back stitch, technique instead of the usual slanting stitches. (4) It was most frequently performed by more experienced needlewomen who were paid for their work. Later, the embroidery was given to the village tailors for further elaboration. Certain elements on the bridal sleeves were also embroidered with silver-gilt thread, after which ready-made silver-gilt braids were attached to the design as well. Some chemises with embroidered sleeves, which also incorporated elements made of silver-gilt thread and silver-gilt braids, were used for determined ritual events, according to which they were called *vodarska,* worn on the first day after

Cvetnici (Palm Sunday), and *kolacharska,* worn when the bride went to her mother's house for the first time after the wedding and brought *kolach,* a kind of pastry. Young unmarried women wore chemises with sleeves embroidered primarily in white. The bottom part of the chemise from Mala Reka was usually embroidered with white cotton threads in parallel and zigzag rows. The needle lace join chikme was also executed with white cotton threads. The embroidered sleeves of the chemises from the Miyak village of Ehloetc in Kicheviya are very similar to those from Mala Reka.

In the Miyak villages of Oreshe and Papradishte, Veles district, the most distant villages of the Miyak migration, several specific features distinguish the chemise sleeves from other Miyak groups. Instead of silver-gilt thread and braids, they were decorated with purchased fine yellow silk cords – *bukme.* In many examples the red and yellow combination is striking even at first glance. (6) The fine motifs bordering the drawn work bands towards the top of the sleeve are also unique. Small rectangular shapes named *pilci* or chicks are most frequently surrounded on all three sides with linear fence lines, called *gradenica;* the entire embroidery design is called *gradeni pilci.* (7) Furthermore, additional motifs known as crosses, *krstovi,* and flags, *bayraci,* were embroidered above them and all the way to the shoulder. These motifs were not used in Mala Reka.

It should be emphasized that the sleeves of the unmarried girls' chemises, known as *poshnavici* in Veles district are entirely void of drawn-work and instead are decorated with horizontal chains of flattened diamonds, *arbalii,* worked in slanted Slav stitch. The sleeves of the chemises for married women could have only one or several horizontal bands with drawn-work embroidery. Some sleeves had additional decorative elements such as krstovi, others had bayraci as well. The bridal chemise was called *ubava* and it was characterized by wider drawn-work bands and the biggest bayraci, as well as the usual pilci, but embroidered with slant stitch unlike those from Mala Reka. The embroidery on the chemise hem in these villages was executed with linen threads dyed a yellowish shade.

The chemise from the Miyak village of Smilevo near Bitola shares some similarities with that of the group from Veles. The sleeve and especially the chest embroidery, *parti,* incorporates fine yellow cords often applied as wavy lines and branched motifs, although to a lesser extent than Veles. (8) The fine finishing embroidery

6) Horizontal detail of page 247

7) Detail of page 246

8) Detail of page 216

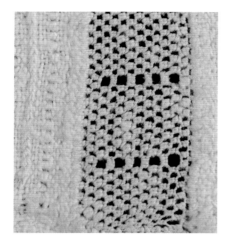

9) Detail of page 222
10) Detail of page 124

and the krstovi motifs at the top of the sleeve are smaller than on the other Miyak sleeves. The drawn-work bands, usually five, are not as wide as on the sleeves from Mala Reka and white is not so abundantly used. The bridal chemise from the village of Smilevo, known under the term of *pisa,* has the characteristic finishing embroidery *pisani pilci* on its sleeves like the corresponding type on the bridal sleeves from Mala Reka. The bottom of the chemise is adorned with embroidery using white linen, cotton, or silk threads.

The Miyak chemise from the city of Krushevo is not significantly different from the one originating in the village of Smilevo. The sleeve of the bridal chemise carried a row of slanting stitches, sindyati, in silver-gilt threads, whereas the sleeves for elderly women had a row of slanting stitches of black threads. The connecting chikme was executed with white, highly twisted, smooth cotton or silk threads; whereas the same white embroidery around the hem, done with thicker silk or hemp thread, creates a 3-dimensional effect. (9)

The ancient Miyak square head pieces – darpni, made of linen cloth were also adorned on all sides with luxurious dark red silk embroidery using a reversible technique. They fell into disuse by all Miyak groups a long time ago. In Mala Reka and the village of Ehloetc, they were replaced with square head pieces made of white cotton cloth, with narrow red embroidered borders. (10) In the village of Smilevo they started wearing several kinds of darpni, mostly made of light cotton cloth. The young wore darpni with silver-gilt embroidery that was worked by Turkish women from the surrounding villages, as well as those which they themselves would embroider with multi-colored floral motifs executed in small cross stitch.

The drawn-work technique, kinatica, used on the Miyak chemise, appears only in isolated cases in the embroidery of other Macedonian garments. There is as well another type of draw-work that was used exclusively on the sleeves and chest of older chemises from Debarsko Pole, Debarska Zhupa, and the city of Debar. In this region, the chemise is characterized by colorful embroidery on the sleeves and chest, as well as white embroidery on the bottom of the skirt. The special drawn-work technique kyesme was unique in Macedonia; its execution required removing both warp and weft yarns from the cloth. Burgundy colored silk threads

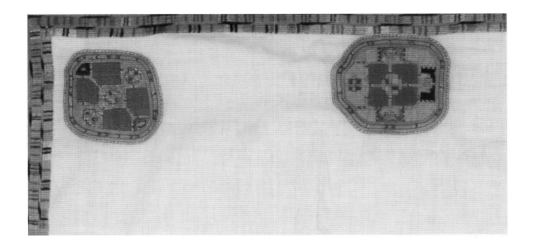

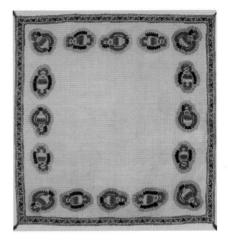

were used for the embroidery, but pink–*shekyerna* became fashionable long ago. Silver-gilt thread was also included. This type of stitching was abandoned in the nineteenth century, replaced by floral motifs and ready-made laces around the hem.

The embroidery design of the large square head piece worn in the Debar region survived for a longer period and it remained in use almost until the middle of the twentieth century. (11) The darpna was characterized by twelve to sixteen oval shapes, *vetki,* evenly spaced around the outer edge. Usually identical shapes were embroidered on the corners while different patterns were used in between. Each vetka is surrounded by a ring of tiny black hooks or spirals–*loza.* They were worked in a double-sided technique–*trupa.* Experienced needlewomen called *pisachki* in the city of Debar would draw the outline on the cloth. Various designs of vetki were used according to the age of the wearer. A bride covered her head with *darpna klabodanliya,* with sixteen vetki, which were also embroidered with silver-gilt thread–*klabodan.* (12/13) The design of the vetki changed as a woman went through life, but they retained the basic principles of arrangement on the scarf and the technique employed was unchanged.

Within the same ethnographic region, two adjacent areas, Debarski Drimkol and Golo Brdo, are linked by similarities of dress. Nevertheless, there is a difference in the embroidery, especially on the sleeves of the chemise. The sleeve from Debarski Drimkol is distinguished by the remarkably unique ornamental structure and specific relief stitch–*skorchi,* which required using tightly twisted woolen threads. The bottom of the sleeve is composed of several variously ornamented horizontal bands, while the upper sleeve has vertical columns called *lozi,* or vines. (14) The sleeves were differentiated by the number of columns as *so tri lozi*–three, *so pet lozi*–five, *so sedum lozi*–seven, and *so devet lozi*–nine. The bridal chemise called tnoka had nine vines–so devet lozi. The dominant color was dark red, formerly derived from the madder plant.

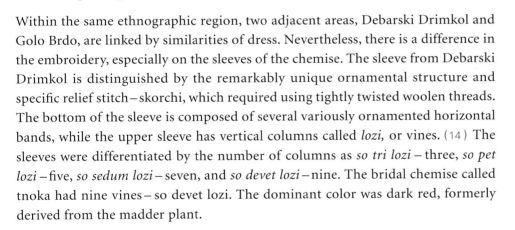

11) Horizontal detail of page 144
12) Detail of page 145
13) Detail of page 145
14) Detail of page 149

In the neighboring region of Golo Brdo, the sleeve embroidery is completely different. It was executed with woolen or silk threads with smooth, flat stitches. The designs were initially outlined with black threads and then were filled with slant stitch. The Golo Brdo sleeve is notable for its distinct ornamental composition formed by two larger parts, whose dominant motif is the specific octagonal star–

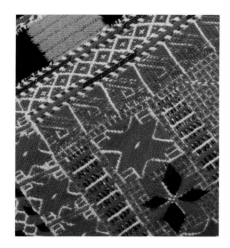

15) Detail of page 156
16) Detail of page 88

petanek.(15) In addition to using burgundy color silk and wool, some sleeves were also embroidered with orange wool, which is also a unique feature of this costume. White stitching on the hem and the seams from both Debarski Drimkol and Golo Brdo is similar to that on the Miyak chemise.

The head scarves from Debarski Drimkol and Golo Brdo also share similarities in the embroidery. Within both of these neighboring groups, women wore small square cloths called korpi which had almost identical ornamental character of four-sided shapes called vetki and little floral motifs called *cvekyinya.* The scarves differ solely in the techniques used; those from Debarski Drimkol were embroidered with the same 3-dimensional stitch seen on the chemise sleeve while korpi made in Golo Brdo use the slanted Slav stitch seen on sleeves from that area. Moreover, both costumes are also related by the same embroidery designs on the chest of the chemise, parti, which are identical in color, technique, and ornament, and are executed on a separate piece of cloth.

In the Upper Vardar ethnographic area, the ensemble from the Kumanovo region is distinguished by its specific embroidery. Older chemises display extensive embroidery on the hem including triangular shapes, *uskuknyak* and delicate branching motifs that extend up the back. The sleeves are embroidered from the edge to the shoulder with heavy use of black. The colored motifs are embroidered on a black background cloth. In the later chemise from this area (page 100) the hem and sleeve decoration has been greatly reduced to a narrow band while the chest embroidery and collar retain more of the older characteristics.

In the neighboring ethnic region of Skopska Crna Gora, a characteristic feature on the woman's chemise is the massive amount of black relief embroidery with subtle dark blue accents. For embroidering, the women used woolen threads in varying thicknesses and degrees of twist to create more or less relief while using various techniques. The hem of the chemise is dominated by vertical columns of embroidery that extend up the back. The middle column called *provezica* is wider, while those on either side of it, named *prukye,* are narrower. The number of columns depends on the age and social status of the individual wearing it. The sleeves are embroidered from the wrist to the shoulder. Two types of sleeve are recognized according to the techniques used and the textured appearance.

In contrast to the intense black relief embroidery in Skopska Crna Gora, in most of the other villages in the vicinity of Skopje, i.e. the ethnic region of Skopska Blatiya, the chemise is entirely different, with its multi-colored embroidery and exuberant ornamental design using woolen and silver-gilt thread. The motifs are marked using the Holbein stitch, obloz, with black thread that is as thick as that used for the slanted Slav filling, polnez. The stitches slant towards each other throughout the motif. The chemise is richly embroidered on the lower portion, on the sleeves, and along the chest opening with leaf like shapes, triangular shapes, and rhomboids as well as other elements.(16) While the color black dominates the work, it is combined with dark red and small amounts of metallic thread, srma. Around the beginning of the twentieth century, women started to decorate the entire lower portion of the chemise with different ornamental combinations and a much greater use of metallic thread. Among them, the most admired was the *gyergyevliya* chemise, embroidered with the distinctive straight branches and the

17) Detail of page 80
18) Detail of page 114

motif called *zelykorka* (a stylized turtle) between them. (17)

Diverging from this colorful ornamentation is the bridal chemise from Skopska Blatiya, known as *crnetica*, or *crnogorka*, embroidered exclusively with black wool. The style was adapted from neighboring Skopska Crna Gora, but with less pronounced relief. The bottom portion of the chemise is decorated with black columns – *pratoi*, most frequently alternating with *provezi* of stacked diamonds or without them. (pages 82 and 83) The sleeves are embroidered from the edge to the shoulder entirely with black wool, similar to the corresponding ones from Skopska Crna Gora.

The chemise from Dolni Polog, in the Polog Valley, is also characterized by black relief embroidery made from thick woolen threads, but in combination with profusion of silver metallic threads, which contributes to its uniqueness. The embroidery design is composed of several horizontal bands on the back of the skirt, and of several vertical columns above them – *provezi*. In contrast to the richly embroidered skirt, the sleeves display only a narrow strip running from the shoulder to the wrist. (page 110)

Work from the cluster of villages at the foot of Suva Gora Mountain within the same Polog Valley is distinguishable by unique embroidered decoration on the woman's chemise that is completely different from its neighbors. The simplest have a border of uniform triangular shapes around the bottom. However, the chemise for festive occasions and marriage ceremonies is distinguished by added large blocks of embroidery – *uskolena*, two on the front and two on the rear, or only two on the front. These blocks are composed of several segments that mirror each other on either side of the seams joining the main garment sections. (18) Along with various other techniques, there is also drawn-work, in these villages called chikme, which is the same word as the Miyak needle lace, executed on a larger scale. The main sleeve embroidery is placed at the shoulder which, in regard to the chemise, is unique in Macedonian village dress. In examining the technique used, it is mostly slanted Slav stitch in both directions.

In the Brsyak ethnographic region, which occupies a large geographical area, the embroidered decoration on women's dress shows many similar general characteristics but with specific differences that identify geographic areas and villages. The

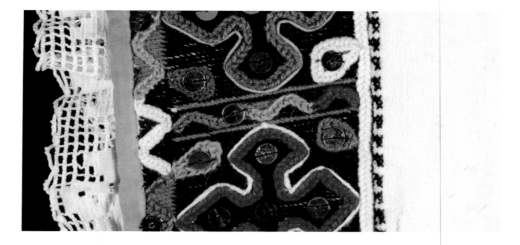

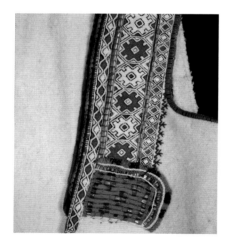

19) Detail of page 199
20) Horizontal detail of page 178
21) Detail of page 200
22) Detail of page 166

embroidered decoration on women's dress shows many similar general character-istics but with specific differences that identify geographic areas and villages. The Bitola-Prilep Plain (Bitolsko-Prilepsko Pole) covers most of the vast Pelagonia Valley. Macedonians living in the valley are known to their mountain dwelling neighbors by the name *polyani*. In general, female dress exhibits rich and varied embroidery, not only on the chemise but also on the outer garments, as well as the luxurious sokay head pieces. Woolen threads, twisted only by hand, were regularly used for embroidery work. The chemise is heavily embroidered at the bottom with a wide ornamental border called *okolno*. On the back there are two elongated rectangles called *boyovi* or *poli*. On the side seams are added a smaller motif, *pobochnik* or *porebornik,* consisting of several circles that are stacked or branched. (19) The sleeves of the chemise are embroidered from the wrist to above the elbows starting with three horizontal bands, the middle one, called *zapest,* being the widest. Above this is the main ornamental composition. The collar and the chest decoration—*prednici,* were executed on a separate piece of cloth.

The embroidery used three main techniques: slanted Slav stitch, horizontal straight stitch, *grabeno,* and satin stitch, *pisano.* Designs called *polneti,* meaning filled in with polnez or slant stitch, and outlined with Holbein were most extensively used. In these instances the stitches always slanted the same direction. The embroidery designs called *grabeni* are created by using groups of horizontal stitches, grabeno, while the *pisani* are characterized by the use of the freer satin stitch, pisano, which served for the composition of circular ornaments. Because of the preponderant use of the color red, the older embroidered chemises were called *alovi,* Turkish for red. At the beginning of the twentieth century, the use of black became more common and the amount of embroidery was reduced. In these newer variations called *kaleshi koshuli,* dark or black chemise, an extra outline of the motifs with thicker white or colored thread added depth and definition, a technique known as *naklavano.* (20)

On the Bitola-Prilep Plain, the outer garment, made of home produced white cotton cloth-*saya,* was also adorned with embroidery. For marriage ceremonies and holidays, it had additional short sleeves worn on the upper arm—*rakavchinya,* em-broidered by using one of the three main techniques. (21) The upper garments, made of thick woolen fabric—*shayak* and *gornitsa* (bridal), are decorated on both sides

of the front opening with appliqués embroidered on a separate piece of cloth. (22)

Considering the high and remote villages in the mountains on the edge of the Pelagonia Valley, the dress of Mariovo women is the closest to that described above for the Bitola-Prilep Plain. Both the layout of the embroidered parts and the techniques used are the same. The most extensively used technique is the slanted Slav stitch, here known as *orano*; named after the stitch used for outlining. It appears in two ways depending on the number of threads covered by the stitch, *podva*, by two, or *potri*, by three. Satin and horizontal straight stitches are used as frequently as orano. The greatest amount of stitch work is on the bottom of the chemise; the rectangular boyovi on the back, the motifs on the sides named *granka*, branches, and the horizontal border covering the entire edge called okolno. (23)

The uniqueness of the Mariovo chemise follows from the customary use of specific motifs as well as how the sleeves are embroidered. However, the most typical is the embroidery design on the sleeves. They are commonly worked only with large slanting stitches, potri—by three. Most striking is the embroidery on the lower portion commonly called *drobnini*, composed of several rows of black stitching with yellow lines interspersed. The main panel is comprised of two sections of motifs elaborated primarily in red. The exception to this typical schema is the most impressive embroidery on the bridal chemise, *crneta*, which is executed entirely in darkest red silk or wool, using the finer podve technique.

Embroidery is also present on the cotton outer garment *sagyiya*, as well as the bridal *gornenik* made of woolen fabric. Pieces of red cloth, *bogasiya*, were purchased and embroidered, then stitched to the front of the garment. Thus, even the actual embroidery appliqués are called *bogasii*. The additional bridal sleeves, *crneti rakavchinya*, are also embroidered over a ready-made red cloth. During festive occasions, the women wore *pisani rakavchinya* with circular motifs on white cloth, similar to those worn in the Prilep Plain. (24)

Female dress of the Upper Villages of Bitola, Gorni Bitolski Sela, are also characterized by certain specifics in the embroidery design. Decoration on the chemise is placed similarly to those already described. The most noticeable difference is the additional outlining of the motifs' contours with a kind of over-embroidery in

23) Horizontal detail of page 193
24) Sleevelets, Mariovo,
   A.2009.15.8v
   The Ronald Wixman/Stephen
   Glaser Collection
25) Detail of page 169

26) Detail of page 176

27) Horizontal detail of page 169

and spindle. The elongated rectangular boyovi are on the back and extend across the seam connected with colorful needle lace chikme. Two other sections of embroidery, *pobochnici,* are placed at the side seams and use the same needle technique. (26) The sleeve embroidery is composed in horizontal friezes—*vrsti,* with motifs arranged in a stepped pattern, hence called *vrsteni rakavi.* Alternatively, the motifs are surrounded by a frame and stacked. (27)

In the Bitola Upper Villages, even the square head scarf, darkma, was adorned with embroidery called *gugan.* Chronologically, three stages of design can be recognized. The oldest darpni were embroidered at one corner with the same style, technique, and colors as the chemise. Subsequently, the embroidery was done in dark red silk threads, using uncounted, freehand stitches. The most recent variations are executed mainly with black or white cotton threads. Embroidery worked on purchased red fabric was applied to the front of the outer garment, shayak, as well as the half-sleeve rakavchinya.

In two neighboring areas, Kicheviya and Poreche, within the Brsyak ethnographic region, the decoration of female dress with embroidery shows great similarities between them. Homespun woolen threads were used for embroidering until the beginning of the twentieth century, after which they started using *fanelka,* factory-made woolen threads. Here there is far less embroidery on the chemise sleeves and hem than what has already been described. The use of yellow wool with accents of red and black is typical of Kicheviya, while the bridal chemise from Poreche, *guvealnica,* was richly embroidered with silver thread and black wool.

Lavish embroidery characterized the older style bridal head covers, sokay and ubrusi, from these villages, which are rarely seen today. The sokay was the wide Macedonian type with embroidered hood. A longer and wider ubrus, which was entirely embroidered with multi-colored silk, woolen, and silver-gilt threads using a reversible stitch, was worn over the sokay. (page 211)

Dress from the region of Zheleznik, located between the Bitola-Prilep Plain and Kicheviya, suffered great changes at the beginning of the twentieth century. Up until that time, the embroidered chemises closely resembled those from the Bitola-Prilep Plain, where the dominant color was red. They were called *alovni koshuli,* red chemises. After the beginning of the twentieth century, influence from Kicheviya

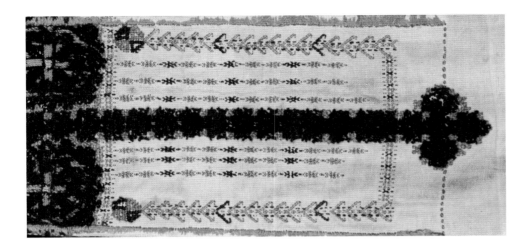

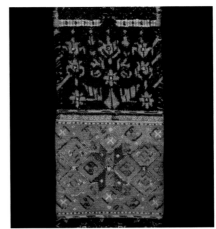

Prilep Plain, where the dominant color was red. They were called *alovni koshuli,* red chemises. After the beginning of the twentieth century, influence from Kicheviya style is noticed with yellow being heavily used. As a result they started calling the chemises *zholti koshuli,* or yellow chemises. The hem of the chemise is adorned in a similar manner as those from Kicheviya, having a narrow border, *okolesh,* and small vertical poli. The sleeve embroidery varies depending on the dominant red or yellow color.

Still within the Brsyak region, several other areas had distinct embroidery traditions. In Strushki Drimkol and Strushko Pole, the chemise was decorated with white embroidery at the hem, while the sleeves bore multi-colored patterns primarily worked in relief stitch, nofteno. Along the edge of the sleeve were borders containing motifs in small squares; a narrow strip of stitching with a cruciform motif on one side ran up to the shoulder. This motif, called *krst* or *perka,* is a unique feature of this area. A later manifestation of the chemise is decorated more modestly with floral cross stitch on the sleeve, as well as the under blouse.

The older style sokay of the Struga area, narrower than the more common Macedonian sokay, were richly embroidered with wool and silk in the relief stitch and straight stitch. (28/29) They did not have a hood with a pointed end like the wider sokay, but a specially formed top resembling a little hat, partially embroidered with motifs on a white background cloth. The sokay were worn in conjunction with a large rectangular head piece – marama, with an embroidered border on one end.

Embroidery from Ohridsko Pole shares certain similarities with the embroidery from the neighboring Struga area. White needle lace is seen at the seams on the bottom of the chemise (30) and the sleeve is adorned with up to three ornamental bands – *zapesti.* Only a narrow embroidered line – *crnka,* proceeds to the shoulder. Wool and silk threads are used, as well as the relief stitch nofteno. Slant stitch is used, both for the sleeves and the native sokay and marami head wear that differ from the previous ones. At one time there was a wide Ohrid sokay with embroidered hood that was abandoned for the Struga style narrower sokay.

In the neighboring area of Gorna Prespa and the city of Resen, the sleeves of the chemise were embroidered with individual square shapes, also called vetki, arranged in a stepped pattern in three horizontal friezes – vrsti, whereas the bottom of the

28) Horizontal detail of page 229
   Detail of page 229
29) Detail of page 229
30) Detail of page 235

In Dolna Prespa, which belongs to the South-Macedonian ethnographic region, the chemise had distinct differences from that of their immediate neighbors in Gorna Prespa. The sleeve embroidery was worked in two larger squares on either side of the seam, joined by colored openwork chikme. This design was abandoned in Dolna Prespa in the beginning of the twentieth century. The bottom of the skirt was decorated with white embroidery and white chikme.

In the ethnographic regions east of the Vardar River, Macedonian women's dress was decorated with much simpler embroidery design and without many local variations. It was characterized by motifs that were more representational and recognizable and sparsely arranged on the white chemise. There was no white embroidery on the bottom of the chemise and the luxuriously embroidered Macedonian head covers were not found here, nor the elaborately embroidered sleeves.

The embroidery on the back of the chemise from the ethnic regions of Radovishko Plain, the eastern part of Slavishte, Piyanec, and others, was usually a pair of individual motifs, *nagorinya, ospolnici, uzboyki,* or *zadnyici.* The sleeves of the chemises worn by the Shopi group in Macedonia were embroidered with two or four individual shapes called *benki.* In Radovishko Plain the outer garment made of white cloth, saya, was also decorated with embroidery. In some places chemises were adorned with woven decoration, *prebir,* instead of embroidery.

The embroidery on Macedonian traditional dress, apart from functioning as the primary identifier of each ethnic region's costume, also emitted various other messages amidst members of specific social groups. Certain embroidered elements, especially on the female chemises, contained signs for marking age and status changes, beginning with the child's chemise, continuing to that of a young girl reaching child bearing age, then a maiden before marriage, a married woman, and finally, that of an old woman. In Mariovo, the young girls' small chemises were decorated with an ornament called *mashko petle,* or cockerel, shaped like a tiny diamond with extended sides, while during puberty with more elaborate ornaments *yagupovi pilinya,* meaning pullet or young hen. In Skopska Crna Gora the status of a girl of marriageable age was indicated by wearing the *provezicharka* chemise, with only one vertical black embroidery design on the skirt back instead of several, and in Dolni Polog, the *retkalche* chemise, with sparse black vertical lines whereas on the bridal chemise they are dense. In Debarski Drimkol, embroidered sleeves with three vines, so tri lozi, were intended for maidens. With the Miyaks in Mala Reka, the maidens wore predominantly white embroidered sleeves, whereas in the Miyak villages of Oreshe and Papradishte, the poshnavici sleeves had no drawn-work on them.

The transition from a maiden into a married woman was symbolically represented by the bridal chemise–tnoka, guvealnica, ubava, or crneta. Each separate social community had its own model of bridal chemise, required and unique for all members of one generation. The older women in Mariovo wore *boraveni* chemises, worked mainly in black and dark red with more white space around the embroidery, and mostly executed in grabeno, horizontal straight stitch. This tradition was also common for those on the Prilep Plain. The signs of mourning in the embroidery design essentially correspond to those denoting old age, and chemises bearing that kind of embroidery were even worn by the young as a sign of grief. In the Bitola Upper

Villages, head pieces with white embroidered gugan were worn as a token of mourning, (31) and in Debarski Drimkol, clothing items were embroidered in a reddish brown called *pitoma*. The bridal chemise was usually kept to serve as burial garb.

The basic components of color, ornament, technique, and other visual signs were intertwined with symbolic and ritually-magical content. In Mariovo, during the ritual *odenye na cheshma* (going to the water fountain) on the Monday after the wedding, the bride dressed in a chemise with the ornament *v'chkata traga*, wolf's paw print or *mechkina dira*, bear's paw print, to ensure that she bear a son. These magical symbols of fertility, related to the wolf and bear cult, were forbidden for use on unmarried girl's chemises. Moreover, only married women in the Bitola-Prilep Plain and Mariovo could wear the pisana chemise (with circular motifs), as well as the embroidered border *tri glavki* (three circular motifs in a triangular pattern) because the circle was associated with fertility and symbolized a new status. In Debarski Drimkol, the *pauni*, peacock, sleeve embroidery design, and in the villages under Suva Gora, the embroidered sleeves called *konychinya* or horses were also restricted to married women. The only time an unmarried woman could wear these designs was when she was engaged to be married, thus transitioning to her new status.

Certain designs, most frequently unfinished embroidery in an unobtrusive spot, functioned as protection against the evil eye, or perhaps a charm to attract the beloved, or as a way to recognize a loved one in the afterworld, *na onoy svet*. Many other ornaments and signs in Macedonian embroidery hark back to the old cultures and civilizations and at one time almost certainly had ritualistic cult symbolism or magical meaning which has long been forgotten but still carry the force of tradition primarily as a decorative element.

31) Headscarf, *darkma*
Gorni Bitolski Sela,
A.2010.6.143
Gift of Bernard W. Ziobro

Skopska Blatiya

I Will Pin this Kiska on My Head[1]

VLADIMIR JANEVSKI

THE CREATION AND EVOLUTION OF MACEDONIAN FOLK DRESS occurred over a long period of time with the earliest indications rooted in the oldest local cultures and connected to religious icons of the people.[2] Indications of this art form in the middle ages are found on frescoes in churches of that period, a notable example in the local church in the village of Psacha, in Eastern Macedonia, and the churches in Ohrid. In the development of Macedonian folk dress we also find Oriental influences introduced by the Ottoman Turks.[3]

Hand in hand with the evolution of the dress went various initiation rituals that were connected to the dress, makeup, and hair of Macedonian women. These rituals are evident even in ancient times and continued as late as the second part of the twentieth century when modern life and western styles overtook the rites that had been practiced through centuries. Among the most practiced rituals were those connected to makeup and hair. They have been documented through folk songs that celebrate the life passage of a young girl to a married woman such as this song from Dolni Polog warning the bride of changes that await her:

> *Say goodbye and cry for your youth,*
> *You will be going to a strange new house.*
> *They will remove your sokaj,*
> *They will unbraid your naplitsi.*
> *You will separate from your large family*
> *Like a sheep from his flock,*
> *Like a wheat stalk from a field,*
> *Like grapes from a vineyard.*

Various beliefs in connection with the hair and head played a great role among the Macedonian people. The head and hair were thought to be sacred, untouchable,[4]

---

1   I would like to thank Menka Aceva Kulevska, born 1922, from the village of Skochvir, who graciously completed the braiding of the model's hair.

2   V. Klichkova, *National Dresses of Macedonia,* (Skopje: Ethnographic Museum, 1963), 3.

3   G. Zdravev, *Macedonian Folk Costumes* (Skopje: Matica Makedonska, 2005), 9.

4   J. Frazer, *The Golden Bough* (Belgrade, 1992, 1ST ed. 1890), 298.

and from there great magical force was attached to them.[5] Additionally the head and hair symbolized the strength and power of the individual.[6] The process of distinguishing boys from girls began at the time a child started walking. In terms of the head and hair, that meant that the boys started wearing caps, while the girls started wearing their hair in braids.[7] Cutting the first lock of hair held a special significance, and from there the mysticism associated with that lock of hair was protected forever. In early childhood the mother began to add various items, like bead decorations, coins, and other things to a child's hair or headwear as protective charms.[8]

The combing and braiding of hair in Macedonia was greatly varied and particular, evident even in ancient times. Every ethnic group had its own specific style of hairdressing.[9] Rituals centered on the hair and head marked changes in status for a female as well. Typically girls would go bareheaded until marriage. As young unmarried women together they started to braid each others' hair, incorporating a multitude of various adornments. As the years passed by, so the hairstyles changed, from day to day providing their own specific and individual message in the communal group. Through the style of dressing one received a message communicating the status of the individual, whether she was a maiden or already a married woman.

In the eleven villages of Skopska Crna Gora north of the capital Skopje, unlike much of the rest of Macedonia, Orthodox Christian girls of marriageable age not only braided their hair in a specific manner but typically wore a head scarf; a sign of crossing over into womanhood. Once a young woman was wed, there were additional rituals that tied the new bride to her new house as her in-laws prepared to present her to the community in her new status as a married woman. These were performed, after the couple returned from the church ceremony, on the first floor of the house where the livestock was kept in the room called *kled*. It started with a ritual called *oplitanje* when the bride bowed in front of the groom ten times. After she did this the groom handed her a water pitcher and she poured water on the hands of the godparents and the best men. Then the unbraiding of her hair began.

As her single braid was undone and rebraided as two braids, and her scarf was replaced with the two head scarves of a married woman, the older women mourned the passing of her girlhood by singing sad songs. The bride cried as the women worked and they consoled her with the song,

> *Girl, oh girl,*
> *Give yourself but don't give in.*
> *Who is braiding your hair?*

---

5 Lj. Radenkovic, *The Symbolic World in Folk Magic of the South Slavs* (Balkanological Institute: Belgrade, Nis, 1996), 25.

6 J. Chevalier and A. Gheerbrant, *Dictionary of Symbols* (Zagreb, 1987, 1st ed. 1969), 293.

7 V. S. Radovanovic, "Folk Costumes in Mariovo," The Newsletter of the Skopje Scientific Society, Books xiv and xv, (1935), 98.

8 G. Zdravev, *Macedonian Folk Costumes, Vol. 1*, (Skopje: Matica Makedonska, 1996), 181.

9 R. Polenkovic-Stejic, *Combing and headscarf covering among the Vlach women in the village of Mezdri*. Tkalicicev Collection, special printing from the first volume, (Zagreb, 1955), 175.

58 *Young Brides, Old Treasures:* MACEDONIAN EMBROIDERED DRESS

When they finished, the bride again poured water to wash their hands and gave a gift of a towel to each woman. On the following day, the bride was taken to the village fountain, by the female members of her new family, to fetch water so she could be introduced to the community and acknowledged as a married woman.

Along with dress and hair style the face was also given much attention, in particular among Muslim women. In five villages outside of Skopje where Macedonian Muslims live, Tsvetovo, Elovo, Drzhlivo, Bela Crkva, and Dolno Kolichani, known as Skopska Torbeshia, a bride was ritually prepared to move to her husband's family home by the application of special makeup by the female members of her new family. First her face was whitened, historically with powdered limestone, *belilo*, and on her cheeks were painted circles of deep red, *tsrvilo*. Then fine metal wire or gold colored paper was pasted on her cheeks by an older woman experienced in the technique. Meanwhile, the other women sang and played a drum called *dajre*. Cries of "she is ours, she is ours, she is ours" were heard from the house of the groom.

Once she was dressed and several other rituals performed, she was taken out of her house and helped to mount a horse waiting to take her to the groom's home. When she was in the saddle she was covered with a white sheet to protect her from the evil eye. The concealing of her face, both with disguising makeup and with cloth, deflected any evil. As a newly married couple both the bride and groom were thought to be vulnerable to the ill wishes and intentions of others that could cause them harm.

A woman continued to use the makeup with which she was painted on her wedding day throughout her life. Repeated trips to a special grocery known as *bakalnitsa* were made where she would buy the makeup, as illustrated in this folk song:

> *The moon lit the road from Salonika to Tetovo.*
> *Ah, but it was not the moon, but three young brides*
> *Three young brides headed to Tetovo*
> *Headed straight to the Uncle Jakim's shop.*
> *Good day, Uncle Jakim,*
> *We're here to buy gram belilo, gram tsrvilo.*
> *Our husbands are gone to work abroad*
> *But they will pay you when they return.*

In another song, young men used the reference to makeup to express their love:

> *Open the door, oh beautiful Lena*
> *So I can see your pretty fair face,*
> *So I can see your face flushed and made up,*
> *So I can kiss your honey soft lips.*
> *I can't come to the door my darling*
> *My mother has fallen asleep on my dress.*
> *So I won't be able to get up*
> *So I can't open the door.*

Or to express trouble in the marriage:

> *Beautiful Maria,*
> *Do not put on rouge.*

Do not powder your face.
Do not dress up.
The neighbors are laughing at me.
Whoever you look at—you wound,
And me, you set on fire with your beauty.

Another practice involving the head and hair of young women was once found in many different communities all over the country. Skillfully twisted lengths of black, red, or white wool served the purpose of providing the appearance of long, extended hair while at the same time acting as an amuletic device that protected the individual against supernatural forces. These adornments were used to indicate the transitional state in preparation for a new status, signifying that a woman was ritually initiated and ready for marriage. They were also worn during the first year of marriage.

These wool extensions had various names, depending on the region or village, such as: *kotsle za devojka,* a false braid for a girl, or *golem kotsel za nevesta,* a large false braid for a bride, in Mariovo. A false braid in the Bitolsko Podmariovski region was called *prtsle* while *prtsle-tilnik* referred to a false braid worn at the nape of the neck in Prilepsko Pole; *til* means the back of the head or nape of the neck. Other names used are *prtsle* in Poreche, Debartsa, Zheleznik and Kicheviya, *piskyul,* meaning tassle, in Skopska Torbeshiya, *kotsel* in Skopska Blatiya and Kumanovsko, *naplitsi,* braids, in Dolni Polog, *pletenitsi* among the Miyaks, and *gaitan,* the word for cord or braid, in Debarski Drimkol. What follows is a specific review of the combing and braiding of the hair of *chupi,* young girls of marriageable age, in the village of Skochvir, in the Brsyak region.

The village of Skochvir lies along the southeastern portion of Bitolsko Pole and borders Mariovo, Bitolsko Pole, and the Moshtenska group of villages in Lerinsko Pole. Formerly, marriage ties were maintained with the surrounding villages of Brod, Dobroveni, Veleselo, Slivinitsa, Polog, Gnilezh, Tepavitsi, Iveni, Baldoentsi, Paralovo, Oreovo, Brnik, and Orle.

In the past this entire area was a crossroads where life was insecure, and various types of looting and plundering occurred regularly. As a result of this instability, the local population was constantly compelled to move and resettle. Over time, these difficult conditions differentiated the populations of Bitolsko Pole, people who lived on the Pelagonia Plain near the city of Bitola, from those in Mariovo, a cluster of villages high in the Nidzhe Mountains. However, the two groups retained some common characteristics that are easily seen in the material culture, and also in the spiritual and intellectual realm, such as the practice and beliefs about dressing the hair. [10]

In the village of Skochvir and the other mentioned villages, the first time a girl's head was covered was on her wedding day. Until the beginning of the twentieth century a married woman covered her head with an *obrus;* after that, women wrapped their heads with a white cotton scarf with embroidered decoration and a tassel, *shamiya so pashka* or *darkma so gugan.*

---

[10] F. Trifunovski, *The Bitola-Prilep Valley, Anthropogeographical Preservation* (Belgrade, 1994), 107.

1)

2)

Most often, hair styles were created by the girls themselves, working with and helping each other. For the most festive occasions, such as large village festivals and religious holidays, the girls started braiding their hair on Thursday or Saturday, so that by the holiday, usually Sunday, their hair would look its best. First the hair was parted; a straight line taken from the nose with the forefinger that went to the back of the head, called the *tilen patets,* where later they braided the *tilnite pletenki,* braids at the nape of the neck. The hair was divided above the ears into sections called *tseluvtsi.* To begin, a lock of hair on either side of the part at the very front of the head was braided. At the top of the braid was attached the *tunturnitsa,* made of black, tightly spun wool yarn in combination with several rows of white beads. This ornament was attached to the braid at the forehead with a metal hook called *yadichka* and at the nape of the neck. The tunturnitsa was worn like this until the beginning of the twentieth century, after which time the girls started wearing bangs and the beaded tunturnitsa was attached directly to the hair, instead of attached with a hook.

The remaining portion of the hair was braided into very tiny little plaits that they gathered all around the ears. Near the ends of these braids they attached *predentse,* twisted wool cords that were usually black but sometimes dark red. (1) These small braids were then divided into three sections. The hair at the nape was made into four or five little braids on each side, which were called *tilnite pletenki.* (2) For the most festive variations young women in Skochvir braided as many as twenty five

little braids while in the neighboring region of Prilepsko Pole the girls braided a similar style using up to sixteen plaits on the sides. [11]

After the small plaits were made they started to braid them into a larger braid. To begin this process, they would braid three plaits from the middle of the bunch and attach an ornament called *niza,* made of pink yarn decorated with a single row of beads. For the most festive occasions they also attached an *oyme,* a triangular ornament made with black and white beads.

Once the niza was braided into place, the rest of the braids were incorporated, in a specific order, into a larger braid that fell down the back. The braid closest to the ear was not included in this bunch but was fastened to either side of the *yalovka,* the term that designates each half of the false hair piece. (3) The woolen threads attached to the ends of the small plaits were also integrated into the larger braid. (4) These intertwined braids, together with the *yazhe,* a group of wool cords that linked the natural hair braid to the prtsle, were about one *peda* (ten inches) long. Then the girl started to braid the tilnite pletenki at the nape of the neck, beginning at the first one closest to the yazhe to the last one in which the yalovki are braided. As the braiding progressed, individual strands of the yarn of the yalovki were added from each side, ending with a braid made entirely of wool.

The entire piece, composed of two yalovki when braided in this manner, was called *prtsle.* On top of the prtsle they would attach another jewelry piece called a *tsela.* Tseli were made by tailors from black, braided cord. Women added additional beads and coin decorations at home. The coins themselves were called tseli in the local dialect, so this entire decorated piece was named after them. The center portion of the tsela was tied to the prtsle.

A chain, hung with silver coins and hooks on each end, called *sindzhir,* was fastened on each side of the apron and draped underneath the hair piece. Finally, a bouquet of natural flowers such as daffodils, tea roses, basil, ivy, or holly was tied together with a red cord and affixed to the hair. (5) With that, a young woman showed she had attained the social status of a *chupa,* a girl ready for marriage. The bouquet, known as *kiska,* was also worn by young brides for about a year after the wedding, pinned to the obrus. The hair style was unbraided in about a month and a woman's best friends started the entire process again. In Macedonia it is well known that adorning oneself with flowers has, according to folk belief, an apotropaic or protective function, [12] while simultaneously symbolizing happiness, joy and health.

Up until the end of the nineteenth century, girls would wipe oil on their hair to give it a high sheen, but later they used only water, because the grease stained their outer garments. A woman braided her hair in this manner her whole life, but as she got older the decorations were left off and the number of braids reduced. This can be verified through photographs from 1913. [13] This style of hair dressing and adornment was maintained until the 1950s.

---

[11]   A. Krsteva, "Macedonian Women's Costumes-Displays of Social Relationships." *Macedonian Folklore,* XXIII/45, Skopje, (1990), 28.

[12]   Z. Nikolova, *Folk Jewelry and Adornments in Macedonia* (Skopje: The Museum of Macedonia, 1982).

[13]   *Macedonia in 1913, Autochromes from the Collection in the Museum of Albert Kahn,* (Skopje: Museum of the City of Skopje, 2001), 106–107.

Although elaborate localized hair styles were not uncommon before World War II, a slow transformation began with the action of the revolutionary committees during the period of the Ilinden Uprising in 1903. The revolutionary leadership forbade the purchase of the dyes and silver-gilt thread needed for embroidered garments, and the purchase of jewelry including the ornaments braided into the hair. They encouraged women to sell their valuables to buy weapons and to show their support for the revolutionary cause by refraining from so-called frivolous activities. According to this testimony from the village of Zhiovo, in the Mariovo area, "The Komitadje did not allow red embroidery or extensive embroidery; they did not allow *krkmi* [bangs] or *kotsle* [additions to the hair]. They would punish our fathers."[14] Many women complied, as demonstrated in this folk song:

> *Yana embroiders a Macedonian flag*
> *She embroiders for three years*
> *And there is no one to ask her*
> *For whom does she stitch those tiny stitches?*
> *Until her aunt finally asks*
> *Say Yana, oh beautiful Yana,*
> *For whom do you stitch those tiny stitches?*
> *Ah my aunt, my dearest aunt,*
> *I am embroidering a Macedonian flag*
> *So I can give it to Jane Sandanski.*[15]

These rituals are not commonly practiced in Macedonia in the present day. There are few women left who remember how to dress the hair or apply makeup in these specific ways. Macedonia became less isolated as the twentieth century progressed and these practices, as well as the making and wearing of dress associated with the female life cycle and particular geographic and ethnic areas, gradually disappeared.

---

14   A.I.F, file 14/5, Mariovo, reg. number 228.

15   One of the most revered Macedonian revolutionary heroes, killed in 1915.

Matka Monastery Church

within the borders of the Republic of Macedonia and the Hellenic Republic

The *Juzhno-Makedonska* (South Macedonian) ethnographic entity mainly within the state borders of Greece, while only a small part is found within the borders of the Republic of Macedonia

Local place names and ethnic designations that were incorporated into these entities specified both geographical area and cultural distinctions recognized by the inhabitants themselves. Toponyms such as *Dolna,* "lower;" *Gorna,* "upper;" *Reka,* "river;" *Pole,* "field;" *Gora,* "forest;" and *Planina,* "mountain," indicate division by altitude and recognition that lifestyle and material culture differed between the high mountain dwellers and those in the river valleys. The people who lived in the mountains were called *Gorani* or *Planinczi* while the valley dwellers were called *Polyani.*

In the mountains, stone and wood were the main building materials for houses. In the lower elevations houses were built from mud bricks or corn stalks and small branches, like willow, with mud. There were distinct differences in how the mountain and valley dwellers dressed.[3] Because the main agricultural activity in the mountains was raising livestock, wool was the main material used for clothing among the mountain groups such as the Miyaks and Shops. The Vlachs were primarily herders as well and used animal fiber such as wool and goat hair for their clothing. In the lower elevations cotton was raised and used primarily to make the clothes, for example the Kotortsi that lived in the area of Ovche Pole and Kochansko Pole in the northeast. Some Brsyaks settled in the mountain area while others settled in the lowlands. For those who lived in the mountains and kept animals, the dominant material was wool, while the lowland Brsyaks whose main occupation was agriculture used cotton.

At the end of the nineteenth century, interaction between different groups was limited to commercial exchange. Even when they practiced the same religion, particular customs and rites were not shared. Intermarriage was prohibited by the rules set by all groups. Marriage patterns defined the actual borders between groups; they were indicators of a sense of belonging and close identification with a birth place or ancestral land. Marriage and family life were vital in maintaining the culture because they reproduced the next generation that preserved the mode of life of the preceding generation. Married couples from the same village or group replicated the model of the community from which they both came. Thus, with limited outside influences, local village culture changed very, very slowly.

Not knowing the other village customs and costumes was often cited as the main reason why the members of one village did not want to marry someone from another place. When the rule was broken, the young were banished and chased out of the village.[4] At the beginning of the twentieth century, there were cases when the community would allow a marriage between individuals of different groups. When this happened, the bride gave up the bridal costume she had spent her adoles-

---

3   A. Svetieva, *Makedonci: materijalna kultura (rakopis)* (*Macedonians: material culture*) *manuscript,* Skopje, 2005.

4   Ibid.

cence making and had to accept the bridal costume given to her by her in-laws. The ethnographic evidence, supported by statistical data, strongly testifies to the existence of an expressed village and group endogamy, that is, the entering into a union with a partner from the same group.

Ethnonyms and exonyms in Macedonia had a very important role in the past. They represented the basis for the collective identification of "ours" and "theirs." Self-assigned ethnonyms were connected to the place in which the group lived or had some connotation of ancient tribal or family affiliation. Exonyms, given to a group by outsiders, were usually connected to some sort of joke so the name often ridiculed the whole group.

The Gornovardarska ethnographic entity encompasses the northern part of present-day Macedonia; the upper reaches of the Vardar River and its tributaries the Lepenets, Pchinja and Kriva Reka. It includes the following areas: Zhegligovo, Sredorek, and the western part of Slavishte, Skopska Blatiya, Skopska Crna Gora, Dolni Polog, Gorni Polog and the five villages at the base of the Suva Gora Mountain. The area of Zhegligovo covers the town of Kumanovo and surrounding countryside. By the end of the nineteenth century the area was populated with Macedonians, Albanians, and Turks while the area of Sredorek, situated east of Zhegligovo, was exclusively Macedonian. [5]

Skopska Blatiya refers to the central part of the Skopje valley. The name comes from the word *blato* meaning mud. Much of the area is a former lake bed. The ethnic makeup in this area was a mixture of Macedonian, Turks, Albanians, and Jews [6] and its center was the city of Skopje. Also in the Skopje valley was the area of Skopska Crna Gora, which was made up of eleven villages in the fold of the mountain of the same name. [7] One village was inhabited by Albanians and the rest were populated by Macedonians.

Within the Polog Valley are the three areas of Dolni Polog, Gorni Polog, and the five villages at the base of Suva Gora. Dolni Polog spans the area around the town of Tetovo known also as Htetovo or Kalkandelen. Since the early years of Ottoman rule Dolni Polog was settled by Turkish colonists. Eventually Tetovo would become an important craft center in Macedonia. Towards the end of the nineteenth century Dolni Polog was mainly inhabited by Macedonians, Albanians and Turks. In Gorni Polog, the main administrative center was the town of Gostivar, in which Macedonians, Albanians and Turkish settlers also lived. [8]

At the turn of the twentieth century there were numerous divisions among people, not just by religion but also by location. Neighbors called each other by derogatory names, for instance *Piskavtsi*, "screamers," was a term used to name the people of a Skopje suburb by the residents of Skopska Blatiya, because they screamed when they

---

5   J. Trifunovski, *Kumanovski kraj*, Seoska naselja i stanovnishtvo (*Kumanovo region*, Rural Settlements and Population), Skopje, 1974.

6   J. Hadzi-Vasiljevich, *Skoplje i njegova okolina* (*Skopje and Surrounding Area*), Belgrade, 1930.

7   S. Tomich, *Skopska Crna Gora*, antropogeografska i etnografska ispitivanja (*Skopska Crna Gora*, Anthropogeographic and Ethnographic Research), Belgrade, 1905.

8   V. K'ncov, *Makedonija:etnografija i statistika*, Izbrani proizvedenija (*Macedonia: Ethnography and Statistics*, Selected Works), Sofia, 1970.

spoke; *Poturi* was a term with a pejorative connotation used for the Macedonian Muslims who lived in Skopska Torbeshija; *Latini* and *Papistani* were terms used for Catholics; *Arnauts, Arnavuts* and *Pljaki* were pejorative terms for the Albanian Muslims. Females in Sredorek, Zhegligovo and Slavishte were called *Belosayki* after the white overcoat they wore while in Dolni Polog, women who wore white head scarves were called *Belokrpki.*[9]

The Debar-Rekanska ethnographic entity spans the westernmost part of Macedonia, south of Korab Mountain, along the confluence of the Radika River and part of the Crni Drim River. Debarski Drimkol, Golo Brdo, Debarsko Pole, Debarska Zhupa, Mala and Dolna Reka, Gorna Reka, and Mavrovsko Pole are located here.

Debarski Drimkol is a small area, situated on the eastern side of the Jablanitsa Mountain. This area was populated mostly by Macedonian farmers or agricultural workers at the end of the nineteenth century. At the beginning of the twentieth century they began to leave for temporary work abroad, mainly due to the harsh economic climate and the looting by bandits known as Kachatsi. The etymology of the name Drimkol is a combination of the name of the river Drim and *kol* which stands for guard, a place where the Turkish authority had placed the gendarmerie to guard the territory. People from the neighboring areas used the exonym *Ketskari,* which means "liars," for the people of Debarski Drimkol[10] and *Uljufi,* "dumb," for the people of Drimkol and Golo Brdo. The inhabitants of Debarski Drimkol called the people in the lower plains Poljani "fieldsmen" or *Shopi* and they in turn, for the people of Debarski Drimkol used the exonym *Tujeshani / Tujki,* because in their speech they used the adverb *tuje/tuka* meaning "here." For the people of Drimkol, the people in nearby Golo Brdo and the Miyaks used the exonym *Obelo* which had a pejorative meaning, because they wore obela, woolen bands wrapped around the lower leg. For the migrants from Albania in Debarski Drimkol the term *Ljushovci* or *Ljush* was used.[11]

Today, the area of Golo Brdo is divided by a state border between Macedonia and Albania, but at the turn of the twentieth century the inhabitants were unified by their common cultural characteristics. The area of Golo Brdo was itself divided into Gorno or Upper Golo Brdo and Dolno or Lower Golo Brdo. The inhabitants were mostly Muslim and Christian Macedonians. The people of Golo Brdo converted to Islam towards the end of the eighteenth century. This relatively recent change allowed the people to still maintain and respect family connections regardless of religious differences. The inhabitants of Gorno Golo Brdo were known as *Planintsi,* "mountain people," and were very similar to the inhabitants of Debarski Drimkol, which suggests that at some point this was one cultural area.

Debarsko Pole is a small valley which is near the confluence of the Radika River and

---

9   G. Petrov, *Materijali po izuchvanieto na Makedonija (Materials Following the Study of Macedonia),* Sofia, 1896; J. Hadzi-Vasiljevic, *Skoplje i njegova okolina (Skopje and Surrounding Area),* Belgrade, 1930; *Makedonija kako prirodna i ekonomska celina (Macedonia as Natural and Economic Entity),* INI, Skopje, 1978.

10   T.D. Florinskij, *Slavjanskoe plemja (Slavic Tribe),* Kiev, 1897.

11   M. Filipovich, *Debarski Drimkol,* Skopje, 1939; *Makedonija kako prirodna i ekonomska celina (Macedonia as Natural and Economic Entity),* INI, Skopje, 1978.

the Crni Drim. At the end of the nineteenth century the area was populated by Macedonians of both Christian and Muslim faith as well as Albanian Muslims. In the years that followed the number of Macedonians decreased because of steady emigration. Regardless of the ethnic or religious affiliation all of them referred to themselves as *Debrani* when outside of Debarsko Pole. However, they recognized clear and distinctive differences among themselves, and when at home the Albanians were *Dibrani,* the Christian Macedonians were *Poljani,* the Turks were *Kadzaklii,* and the Macedonian Muslims were called *Kurki.*

The area of Debarska Zhupa is a small area within the Debarsko-Rekanska ethnographic entity which the locals called Dzupa and they too differentiated between Gorna and Dolna Dzupa. During the nineteenth century and at the beginning of the twentieth century the population was made up of Christian and Muslim Macedonians, Turks, and Albanians and they were all called *Zhupanci, Dzupanci* or *Zhupjiani.* The Turks referred to themselves as *Turkler,* but referred to the Muslim Macedonians as *Torbeshlar,* for the Christian Macedonians they used the term *Kaurlar* (non-believer) and for the Albanians, *Arnautlar.* The Macedonian Muslims identified themselves as *Turci* (Turks). For the Christian Macedonians they used the terms *Kauri, Risyani* (from Chrisyans or Christians), or *Polyani,* and for the Albanians they used the terms *Arnauti* or *Turci.* The Christian Macedonians referred to themselves as *Kauri, Risyani,* or *Polyani,* but when outside of their area they referred to themselves as *Debrani.* For the Macedonian Muslims they used the exonyms *Torbeshi* or *Kurki,* and they referred to the Turks as *Asli Turci* (real Turks), and to the Albanians as *Turci—Arnauti.* [12]

The area of Reka extended alongside the rivers Radika and Mala Reka. During the period of Turkish rule, the administrative center in the area was Zhirovnica. Even though this was a relatively small area, the population was heterogeneous. The area was known as Gorna Reka, Golema Reka, Dolna Reka, and Mavrovo, which indicated internal distinctions. Mala and Dolna Reka were inhabited by Miyaks who worked abroad and referred to themselves as *Nashintsi,* "us/ours." [13] Gorna Reka, situated in a mountainous area east of the Korab Mountain, had a population composed of Macedonians who spoke Macedonian, Macedonians known as *Shkreti* who spoke the Albanian language, and ethnic Albanians. Because of the intense violence and looting that was endemic in this area during the late nineteenth century until the end of World War I, farming became very difficult. As in many of the rural areas, particularly in western Macedonia, people began to emigrate abroad in large numbers. Next to the area of Gorna Reka is the Mavrovo Pole, which encompassed four villages with populations whose main cultural characteristics were very similar to those of the Gorna Reka ethnographic area. [14]

---

12   T. Smiljanich, *Debarski Poljani i Rekanci (Poljani and Rekanci from Debar),* NS, XIII, Zagreb, 1934, 59–76.

13   T. Smiljanich, *Plemenske odlike Mijaka (Tribal Characteristics of the Miyaks),* NS, XIII, Zagreb, 1924, 61–64.

14   T. Smiljanich, *Mijaci, Gorna Reka i Mavrovsko Polje (Miyaks, Gorna Reka and Mavrovsko Pole),* SEZb, XXXV, *Naselja i poreklo stanovnishtva (Settlements and Origin of Population),* bk. 20, Belgrade, 1925, 1–122; D. Nedeljkovich, *Gornorekanska etnopsiholoshka grupa (The Gorna Reka Ethno-Psychological Group),* Journal, SND, IX, Skopje, 1934, 83–129; T. Smiljanich, *Debarski Poljani i Rekanci (Poljani and Rekanci from Debar),* NS, XIII, Zagreb, 1934, 59–76; D. Nedeljkovich, *Mavrovska psihichka grupa (The Mavrovo Psychic Group),* Journal SND, VII–VIII/ 3–4, Skopje, 1930.

The Brsyachka ethnographic entity encompasses the largest part of Western Macedonia and is almost entirely inhabited by Macedonians of the Brsyak tribe.[15] This ethnographic entity includes the areas of Strushki Drimkol, Strushko Pole, Ohridsko Pole, Malesiya, Debarca, Prespa, Zheleznik, Kicheviya, Azot, Poreche, Prilepsko and Bitolsko Pole, Mariovo, and Tikvesh.

The area of Strushki Drimkol spans the eastern slopes of the Jablanitsa Mountain. The neighboring Strushko Pole is situated parallel to it on the other side of the Crni Drim River. By the end of the nineteenth century, the population in the area was made up of Christian and Muslim Macedonians, Albanians, Turks, and Vlachs.[16] Malesiya was a small mountainous area and was populated entirely by Orthodox Macedonians.[17]

Debartsa is a woodland area located northeast of the city of Ohrid on both sides of the Sateska River. In the nineteenth century Debartsa was a nahiya, the smallest Ottoman administrative unit, within the Ohrid kaza; all of the villages in the area were Macedonian except for the village of Pesochani which was inhabited by Albanians.[18] Ohridsko Pole, together with the villages on the coast of Lake Ohrid, lies on the northeast and east shores of Lake Ohrid. The population here was mostly Macedonian, while in the city of Ohrid, Turks, Albanians, Roma, and Vlachs lived alongside Macedonians. City dwellers were typically craftsmen and merchants.[19]

East of Ohrid is the region of Prespa, divided culturally in three parts: Dolna, Gorna, and Mala Prespa. The area today is divided within three political states: Macedonia, Albania, and Greece. According to sources obtained by researchers during the nineteenth and early twentieth century, the makeup of the Prespa population was heterogeneous. Macedonians, Turks, Albanians of the Tosks tribe, Vlachs, and Roma lived here together.[20]

Zheleznik is a mountainous area also known as Demir Hisar. It is divided into Dolni Zheleznik, bordering Bitolsko Pole, and Gorni Zheleznik, also known as Krasta, which borders Kicheviya. The inhabitants here were mainly Macedonians.[21] Kicheviya is situated north of Zheleznik, and even though it was culturally homogenous, the people distinguished between several areas: Gorno and Dolno Kichevo, Gorna and Dolna Kopachka, Rabetino, and Zayas. North of Zayas, alongside the Taymishka River, several Shopski villages were dispersed that had similar cultural characteristics to the people of Gorni Polog from the Gornovardarska ethnographic area. There were Miyak oases in the city of Krushevo and the village of Smilevo, as well as the village of Ehloetc in the northwestern part of Kicheviya. Macedonians were the majority population until the beginning of the nineteenth century, when

---

15   T. Smiljanich,– Bradina, *Pleme Brsjaci (Brsjaci Tribe)*, ns, x, Zagreb, 1931, 81–95.

16   V. K'nchov, *Makedonija:etnografija*, 1970; J. Trifunovski, *Ohridsko-strushka oblast (Ohrid-Struga Area)*, sezb, sanu, Belgrade, 1992.

17   Rusich, B., *Malesija*, gzffus, Historical-Philological Department vi/1, Skopje, 1953.

18   J. Trifunovski, *Ohridsko-strushka oblast*, 1992.

19   Ibid.

20   V. K'nchov, *Makedonija:etnografija*, 1970; G. Trajchev, *Prespa*, Macedonian Library, Sofia, 1923, 3–5.

21   *Makedonija kako prirodna i ekonomska celina (Macedonia as Natural and Economic Entity)*, ini, Skopje, 1978.

APRON. *futa*. Western Macedonia, c. 1920. FA.1969.43.7 CE
Macedonian Muslim. Wool, 29¾ x 20⅞ in. IFAF Collection.

a combination of Albanian in-migration and Orthodox Christian conversion changed the balance.

Poreche is an enclosed valley situated in the middle Treska River valley; the people divided into those of Gorno and Dolno Poreche. The populace was mainly Macedonian, and the main administrative center in the past was the village of Samokov and later the city of Brod.[22] East of Poreche was the mountain area of Azot, which to the north reached the southern parts of the Skopje Valley. The people were Macedonians of Christian and Muslim faith, but there were also Turks and Albanians living there. The Miyak villages of Oreshe and Papradishte are in this area.

Prilepsko and Bitolsko Pole are part of the vast Pelagonia Valley. It is probable that in the past there were many more similarities between the two areas but towards the end of the nineteenth century, differences began to emerge in how people dressed and in terms of spiritual culture. Main administrative centers were the

---

22   P. Jovanovich, Poreche, sɛzb, ʟɪ, *Naselje i poreklo stanovnishtva* (*Settlements and Origin of Population*), bk. 28, Belgrade, 1935.

cities of Bitola and Prilep, and while the Macedonian populace was the most numerous, Turks, Albanians, Jews, and Vlachs lived there as well.[23] The Vlachs arrived in this area after the city of Moskopole was destroyed by the infamous Ali Pasha Yaninski in 1788 and mostly settled in the cities of Bitola and Krushevo; but they were also found in the nearby villages of Gopesh, Nizhepole, Magarevo, Trnovo, and Maloishte on the lower slopes of the Baba Mountain.

One of the larger mountainous areas in the Brsyachka ethnographic entity was the region of Mariovo that spans the lower Crna Reka and encompasses about thirty villages inhabited by Macedonians. Adjacent to the area of Mariovo was the area of Tikvesh, dominated by Macedonian Muslims known as *Dilsazi*, which meant people without a language, because they declared themselves as Turks but did not speak Turkish. After the Balkan Wars of 1912 and 1913 many *Dilsazi* left for Turkey with the retreating Ottoman troops.

The Shopsko-Bregalnichka ethnographic entity is part of the larger Shopska area which extends across the present day borders of Bulgaria and Serbia. This ethnographic entity is comprised of the regions of the Eastern part of Slavishte, Radovish Shopluk, Maleshevo, Piyanets, Durachka Reka, and Ovche Pole. The Shopi, like the Miyaks and Brsyaks, are descendants of ancient tribal people.

The eastern part of Slavishte is comprised of several villages alongside the Kriva Reka, very near today's Bulgarian border. Towards the end of the nineteenth century the population was Macedonian and the main occupation was farming. Within this ethnographic entity are also the border villages in Bulgaria, including the city of Kustendil, as well as a large number of villages in southeastern Serbia. The neighboring area of Durachka River is a small mountainous terrain on both sides of the river. These several villages are administered by the city of Kriva Palanka, as is the eastern part of Slavishte. The population was Macedonian and the main occupation besides agriculture was *valavicharstvo*, the washing of heavy wool bedding used in the households. Women were called *Crnodzupki*, based on the garment *dzube*, which is a black sleeveless overcoat they wore. [24]

Piyanets is a large mountainous region in the extreme northeastern part of Macedonia. At the end of the nineteenth century, the people living here were Christian and Muslim Macedonians known as *Pomatsi*. Vlachs, Turks, and Roma also lived here.[25] Maleshevo is a mountainous terrain culturally similar to its neighbor Piyanets and today spans the border of Bulgaria. The inhabitants of Maleshevo were Christian and Muslim Macedonians and Roma.

The Ovche Pole, "Sheep Field," is a vast area in the eastern part of Macedonia also known as Kotoriya. Culturally, aside from the valley of the same name, Ovche Pole includes the Ezhovo or Shtipsko Pole, the Kochansko Pole, part of the area of Lakavica, and the area around the city of Kratovo. The people here were mostly Macedonians and were called *Kotorci* by the neighboring Shopi. There were also

---

23   T. Smiljanich, – Bradina, *Pleme Brsjaci,* 1931, 81–95; J. Cvijich, *Osnove za geografiju i geologiju Makedonije i Stare Srbije* (*Basics of Geography and Geology of Macedonia and Old Serbia*), III, Belgrade, 1911.

24   G. Zdravev, *Makedonski narodni nosii I,* 1996.

25   J. M. Pavlovich, *Maleshevo i Maleshevci* (*Maleshevo and the Maleshevo Population*), Belgrade, 1928.

Turks and Vlachs living here. The Vlachs were concentrated in the city of Shtip but were also found in several villages in the Ovche Pole region. They belonged to a group called *Karaguni,* based on the black upper garment they wore known as *guna.*

The Strumo-Mestanska ethnographic entity encompasses the eastern part of Macedonia, between the Struma and Mesta rivers and includes parts of the Pirin area that today lies within Bulgaria. To the south, it reaches the Aegean Sea within the border of present-day Greece. Only the areas of Strumitsa and the Radovishko Pole are within the territorial borders of the Republic of Macedonia. The main administrative center was the city of Strumitsa. The inhabitants were Macedonians, Roma, Turks, and the Turkish sub group *Jurutsi.*[26] The Radovish Shopluk is a small Shop oasis comprised of seven villages situated on the southwestern slopes of Plachkovitsa Mountain near the city of Radovish. Shopi from the north moved into this area at the end of the nineteenth century.

The largest part of the Southern Macedonian ethnographic entity lies within the state borders of Greece. There are four villages in the Republic of Macedonia: Bach, Zivojno, Sovich and Germiyan, and part of the area of Boymiya, around the city of Gevgeliya. The inhabitants of Boymiya included Macedonians, Turks, Vlachs, and Roma.[27]

Today, the village women in Macedonia no longer wear local dress; only the oldest women wear an apron and a head scarf on a daily basis. Cultural and religious celebrations and rituals are still found in remote villages and small towns but they are slowly being forgotten. In the cities, the old ways have been abandoned and modern fashion quickly prevailed over whatever remnants of local dress styles the new inhabitants brought with them. Some villages, specifically those in the Mariovo region and along the shore of Lake Prespa, have been emptied by successive waves of migration to Western Europe, the United States, Canada, and Australia as well as urban areas within the country. Still, the majority of Macedonia's villages are inhabited. In Macedonian cities the names of some neighborhoods correspond to the place origin of the earlier immigrants; evidence of patterns of settlement that maintained village associations. Figures from the 2002 census record a population of 2,022,547 of which 64.2% (1,297,981) are Macedonian, 25.1% (509,083) Albanian, 3.9% (77,959) Turkish, 2.7% (53,879) Roma, .5% (9,695) Vlach, 1.8% (35,939) Serbian, .8% (17,018) Bosnian, and 1% (20,993) other.[28] The Republic of Macedonia remains a multiethnic, multireligious nation.

26   V. K'nchov, *Makedonija:etnografija,* 1970.

27   K. Penushliski, *Narodnata kultura na Egejska Makedonija (Folk Culture of Aegean Macedonia),* Skopje, 1992; T. Simovski, *Naselenite mesta vo Egejska Makedonija (Townships in Aegean Macedonia),* Skopje, 1978.

28   http://www.stat.gov.mk/english/glavna_eng.asp

Map showing the ethnographic areas of Macedonia used in the classification of dress. Borders shown as dotted lines on all of the maps are approximations.

The Macedonian Arts Council, from 2007–2010, presented as a gift to the Museum of International Folk Art 25 ensembles of multiple pieces. While a small number of the pieces were purchased, the majority of the costumes were donated to the Arts Council by collectors based in the United States and Macedonia.

Young Brides, Old Treasures:
MACEDONIAN EMBROIDERED DRESS

BOBBIE SUMBERG
VLADIMIR JANEVSKI

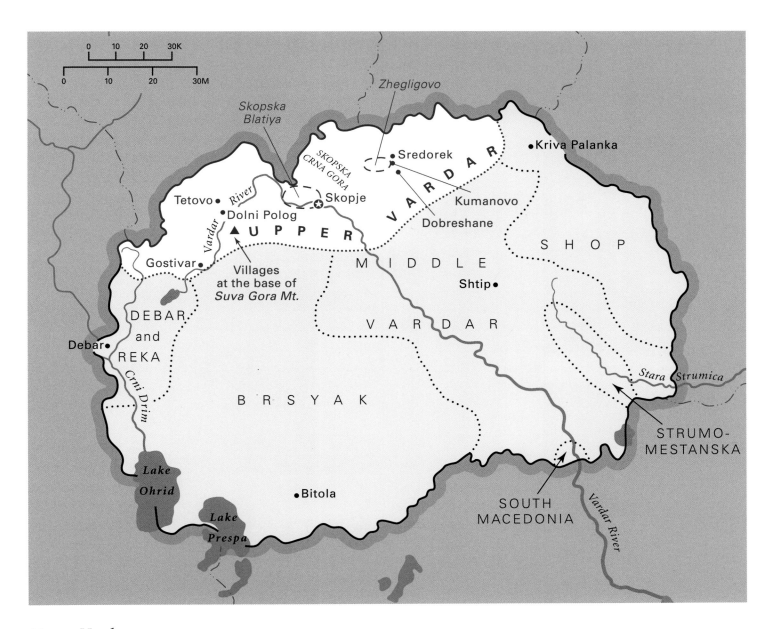

Upper Vardar

The Upper Vardar region (Gornovardarska) encompasses most of the northern part of the country, including the areas of Skopska Crna Gora and Skopska Blatiya in the present-day municipality of Skopje and Zhegligovo and Sredorek in Kumanovo municipality, and extending west to the Albanian border. The population is ethnically and religiously diverse, with Orthodox and Muslim Macedonians, ethnic Albanians, Vlachs, and Roma all living in the region. Although the clothing that people in the region wear shares some features, there are also specific differences. Skopje was an important administrative center during the early Ottoman era. Even though the name *Skopska Blatiya* refers specifically to the low-lying plain on the east bank of the Vardar River, the style of dress worn there was also worn by people living in a much larger area ranging from the western bank of the river and the highlands above it to the hills between the Vardar and Treska rivers.

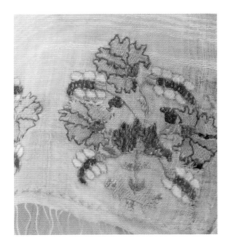

WEDDING DRESS. Skopska Blatiya, c. 1910

Cotton, wool, metal, metallic thread, silk, plastic, glass beads. Gift of Bernard W. Ziobro, The Ronald Wixman/Stephen Glaser Collection, IFAF Collection, Gift of the Macedonian Arts Council. This ensemble features a chemise with colorful and metallic embroidery. The model also wears two sleeveless wool jackets called *elek*. The *elek* replaced an older garment called *saya*. Although both unmarried and married women regularly wore the *saya* until the early twentieth century, it remained in use longer as a special occasion garment. Women living further east in the Shop region wore the *elek* as well, a garment that probably developed from the *yelek*, a sleeved or sleeveless jacket that was worn in Ottoman Turkey since at least 1618.[1] The head scarf, or *krpa,* is an example of Ottoman embroidery, which often decorated towels, sashes, and other types of clothing and textiles in the Empire.

[1] Jennifer Scarce, *Women's Costume of the Near and Middle East* (London: Unwin Hyman Ltd, 1987), 53.

WEDDING DRESS. *crnetica.* Skopska Blatiya, c. 1900

Cotton, wool, metal, metallic thread, linen, silk, glass beads. Gift of Bernard W. Ziobro, The Ronald Wixman/Stephen Glaser Collection, IFAF Collection. The ensemble is named after the black-embroidered chemise, or *koshula crnetica,* which was adapted from the chemise worn in neighboring Skopska Crna Gora. The other elements, such as the sleeveless wool coat decorated with pompoms, the apron, and head scarf, are typically Skopska Blatiya style. The bridal coat or *kyurdiya* has more rows of red pompoms than would the *kyurdiya* worn by a recently married or older woman. A bride would deliberately wear the apron pooched out so that she appeared to be pregnant.

COAT. *kyurdiya.* Skopska Blatiya, c. 1910. A.2010.6.21

Wool, cotton, metal, glass beads, 36¼ x 22 ⁷⁄₁₆ in. (92 x 57 cm). Gift of Bernard W. Ziobro. A newly married woman wore this style during her first years of marriage.

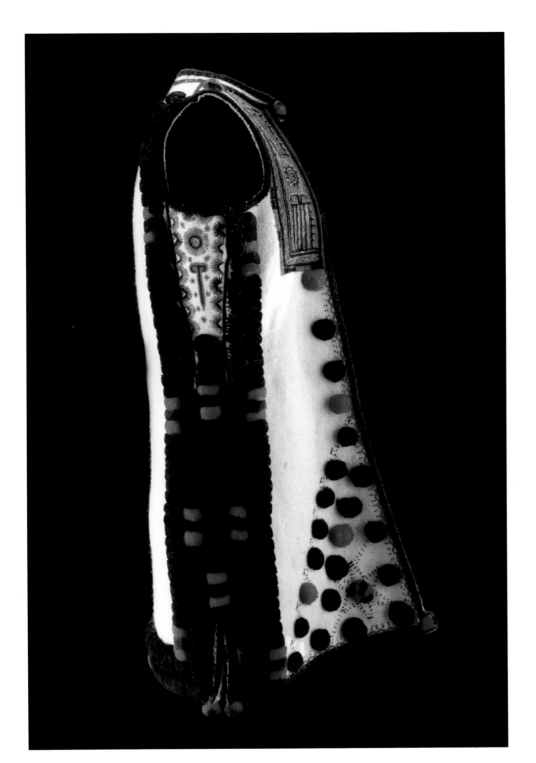

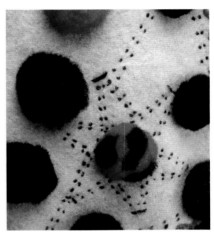
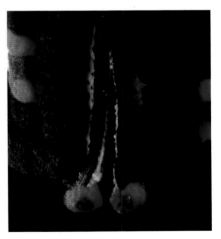

COAT. *kyurdiya.* Skopska Blatiya, c. 1900. A.2008.7.53

Wool, silk, metallic thread, 36 x 13 in. (91 x 33 cm). The Ronald Wixman/Stephen
Glaser Collection. Older women wore a sleeveless coat like this one, more soberly
ornamented than that of the bride or newly married woman.

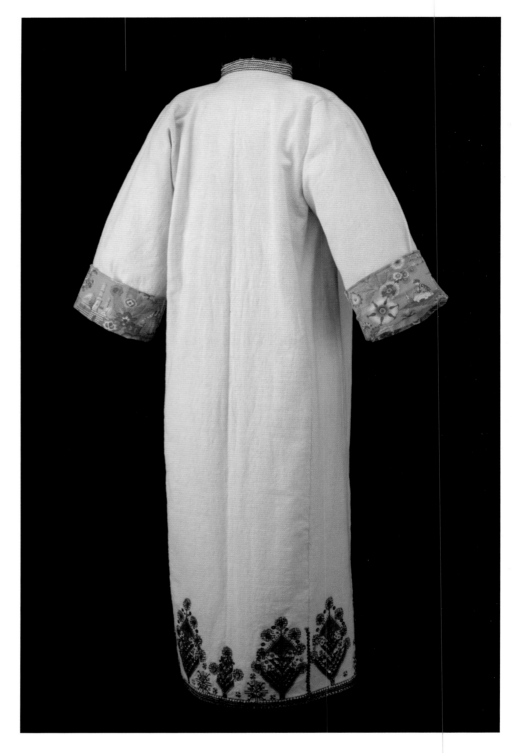

CHEMISE. *gyergevlia koshula.* Skopska Blatiya, c. 1920. FA.1972.26.1a

Cotton, wool, metallic thread, sequins, length 50¹³⁄₁₆ in. (129 cm). IFAF Collection. An older style of Skopska Blatiya chemise was embroidered with black, red, and metallic thread, *srma,* as is seen on the front opening. Lush geometric patterns using the same colors were placed on the sleeves and on the hem. The *gyergevlia* chemise combines the older embroidery style on the chest with the newer multi-colored work on the hem. The printed cotton lining of the sleeve shows a romanticized bit of Turkey.

GIRL'S DRESS. Skopska Blatiya, c. 1980

Cotton, wool. IFAF Collection. Radka Spasoska of Bulachani, a village in Skopska Blatiya, made this outfit for her daughter, who wore it when she was eight years old.

NEW GROOM'S DRESS. Skopska Blatiya, c. 1920

Cotton, wool, leather, glass beads. IFAF Collection, Gift of Bernard W. Ziobro, Gift of Mr. and Mrs. William F. Hennessey. A man wore this ensemble, a shirt, *ayti,* vest, *elek,* trousers, *gakyi,* belt, *poyas,* hat, *shubara,* and towel, *krpa,* on his wedding day with the addition of a *jube* or sleeveless coat normally only worn by a man in his fifties or older. A young man not yet married wouldn't have to wear the vest or hat. Although men's dress was less status-specific than women's, it was sometimes used to express change.

COAT. *jube.* Skopska Crna Gora, c. 1900. A.2010.6.132

Wool, 34 ¼ by 20 ½ in. (87 x 52 cm). Gift of Bernard W. Ziobro. Men and women both wore this type of sleeveless coat in the villages in the Crna Gora Mountains outside of Skopje.

BELT ORNAMENT. *kustek.* Skopska Blatiya, c. 1920. FA.2008.23.20

Glass beads, metal coins, length 14 ³⁄₁₆ in. (36 cm). IFAF Collection. Both men and women wore the *kustek* around the neck or tucked into the belt. The attached coins make this a woman's piece. The Ottoman coins are dated 1223, which according to the Gregorian calendar is 1808.

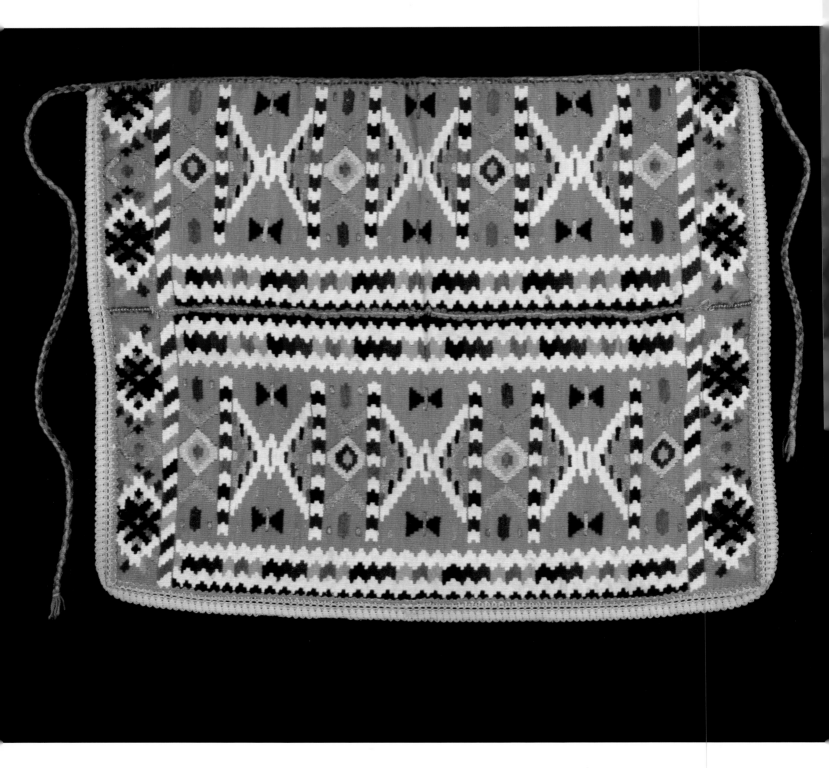

APRON. *vuta so tri kola.* Skopska Blatiya, c. 1920. A.2008.7.54

Wool, cotton, metallic thread, 25 x 30 5/16 in. (63.5 x 77 cm). The Ronald Wixman/ Stephen Glaser Collection. *Vuta so tri kola* means "apron with three kola" or diamond motifs also called wheels. It was woven in two sections, each with three major motifs, and joined with a horizontal seam. Machine-made lace was sewn around three edges.

WEDDING CAP ORNAMENT. *tas.* c. 1900. FA.1972.26.1

Silver, coins, glass, plastic beads, diameter 5 ½ in. (14 cm). IFAF Collection.

APRON. *peshkir edinicharen.* Zhegligovo, c. 1920.

Wool, metallic thread, 29 ¾ x 28 ¾ in. (75.5 x 73 cm). Gift of Bernard W. Ziobro. The use of metallic thread indicates that this is a wedding apron, and a newly married woman would wear it on Sundays until she had her first child.

WEDDING DRESS. Zhegligovo, c. 1920

[Details of Following Spread] Cotton, wool, metallic thread, metal, glass beads. Gift of the Macedonian Arts Council, Gift of Bernard W. Ziobro, Museum Purchase. The bride's fitted vest, seen in the detail, is called *saya.* A woman wore it for the first year after her wedding. On her forehead are imitation coins made from brass and tin called *tontuzi.* An older chemise from the nineteenth century would have had much more embroidery on the hem and sleeve; the entire wedding ensemble was more elaborate then, indicating the tendency to simplification as the twentieth century progressed.

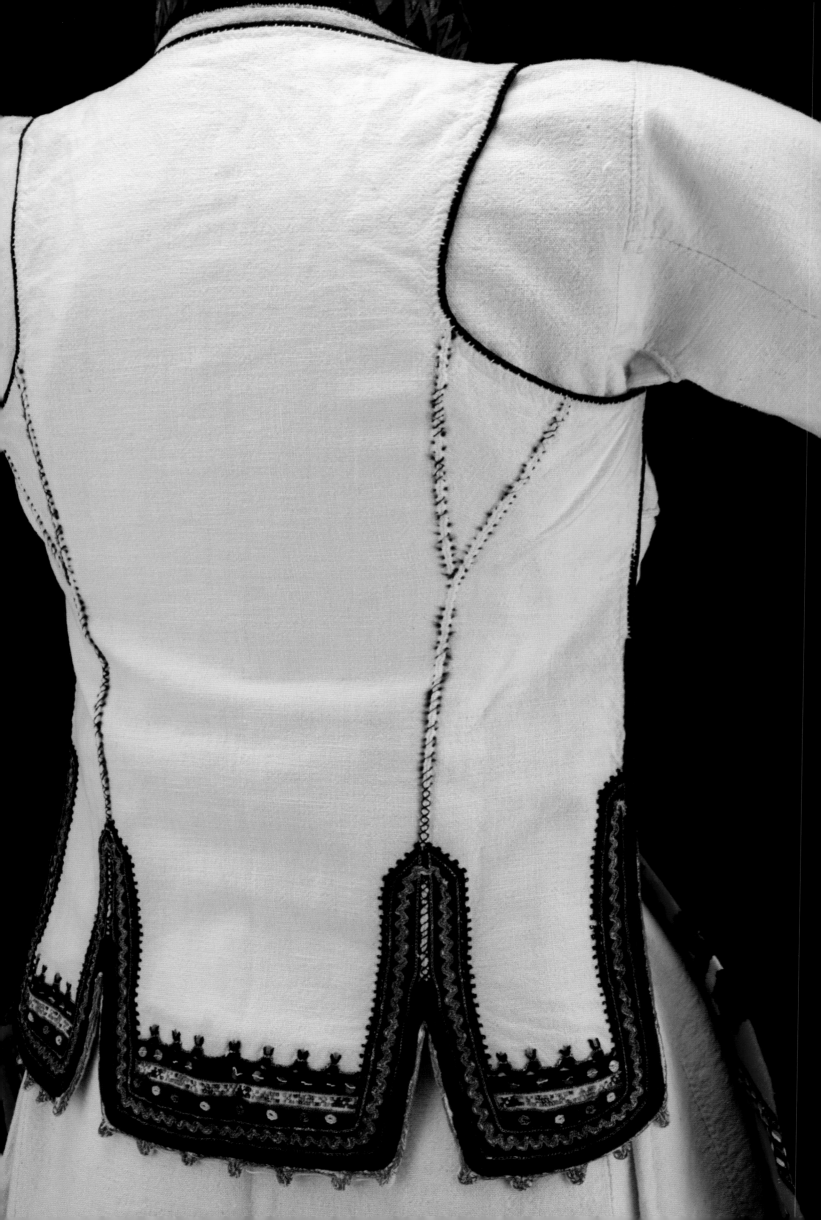

SOCKS. *perpoci di harsafi.* Vlach, c. 1870. FA.1972.26.3E

Wool, metallic thread, length 19 5/16 in. (49 cm). IFAF Collection. Vlachs, also known as Aromanians, speak a Latin-based language. Thus the terminology for garments is entirely different from the Macedonian terms. Harsafi means "metallic thread."

NEW BRIDE'S DRESS. Karaguni Vlach, Kumanovo municipality, c. 1930

[Detail of Following Spread] Wool, cotton, metal, hair, glass beads, silk, metallic thread. Gift of the Macedonian Arts Council, IFAF Collection. The beaded dickey, *keptar,* visible at the neck goes on first. Underneath the visible clothing on this mannequin are a plain cotton chemise, *kmesha,* a long-sleeved velvet jacket called *mintan,* and over that a very heavy red and black plaid wool jumper called *fusta.* The black velvet band sewn to the bottom of the skirt is the only part of the *fusta* that shows. Next comes a pleated, black, wool *k'ndusha,* sleeveless coat, with red trim on the bodice, a beaded belt, *brno di mrzyali,* an apron with metallic thread, *poala,* and another long-sleeved velvet jacket, *libade.* The hat is placed on the head, a red scarf, *kavrak,* rolled and tied in place, and the *amuri,* a beaded band, is tied on.

HAT. *k'chula.* Karaguni Vlach, Dobreshane, Kumanovo municipality, c. 1930.
FA.2010.63.1

Wool, hair, metal, metallic thread, glass beads, height 5 ¹¹⁄₁₆ in. (14.5 cm). IFAF Collection. The braid provides a base to attach the band of bead ornaments on the crown of this hat. If a young woman had thick long hair, she would braid it and wrap it around the hat. If she didn't, a braid of someone else's hair was attached, as in this example. After her marriage, a new bride wore only a plain yellow head scarf, except on special occasions.

APRON. *poala*. Karaguni Vlach, Kumanovo municipality, c.1890. FA.2008.23.5

Wool, 23 ⅝ x 13 ¾ in. (60 x 35 cm). IFAF Collection. An older woman of this ethnic community would wear this apron.

SOCKS. *perpoci di harsafi*. Karaguni Vlach, Kumanovo municipality, c.1930 A.2010.77.7ab

Wool, metallic thread, length 20 ¾ in. (52.5 cm). Gift of the Macedonian Arts Council.

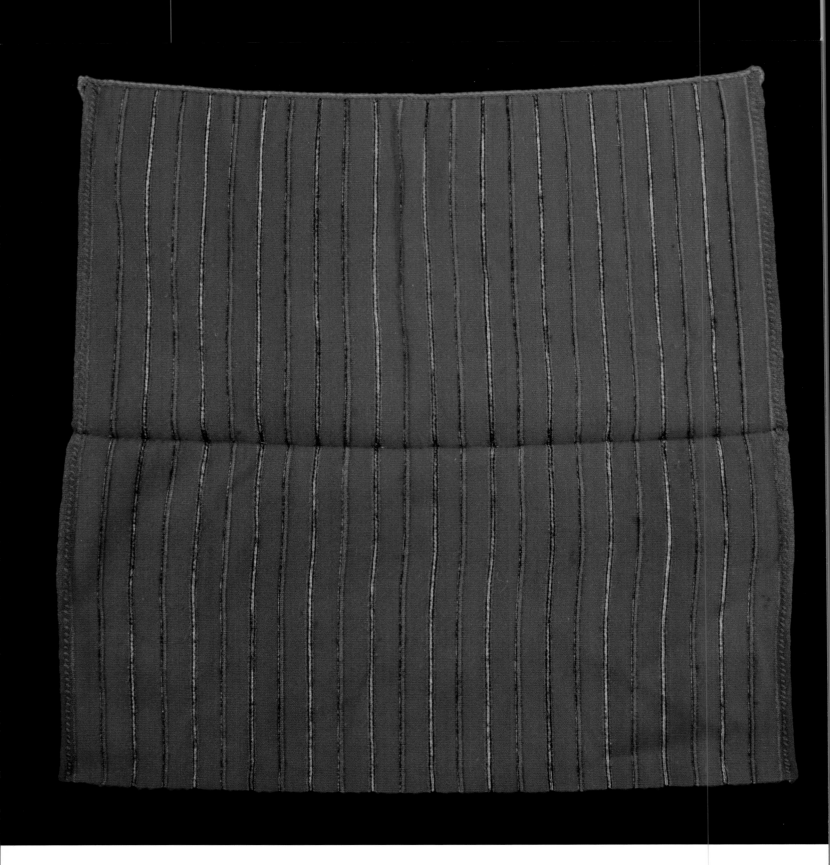

APRON. *zaviatchka.* Dolni Polog, c. 1910. A.2010.6.64

Wool, 25 ³⁄₁₆ x 25 ⁹⁄₁₆ in. (64 x 65 cm). Gift of Bernard W. Ziobro. Women wore plain striped aprons like this one every day.

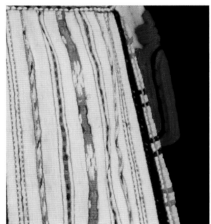

NEW BRIDE'S DRESS. Dolni Polog, c.1910

[Details of Following Spread] Cotton, wool, rayon, metallic thread, metal, glass beads, paper. Gift of Bernard W. Ziobro, Gift of the Macedonian Arts Council. A blouse, whose lower sleeves and ruffled front show, was worn under the chemise. It has the same shape and name, *koshulche,* as that worn in the villages at the foot of Suva Gora Mountain. The lines of black embroidery on the back of the chemise are 13 in. long. They were stitched with thick wool yarn in a technique that created relief. The density of the lines indicates that this garment is a bridal chemise that a newly married woman would have worn on Sundays and feast days for the first few years after her marriage. The chemise typically has metallic thread work, the amount reflecting the wealth of the bride's family. A bride would have worn more jewelry at the wedding, as well as different headwear. A large, vertically striped apron, *zaviatchka,* is worn over a smaller, horizontally striped apron, *skutinche.*

YOUNG WOMAN'S FESTIVAL DRESS. Villages under Suva Gora, c.1900

Cotton, wool, metallic thread, metal, glass beads, silk, possibly synthetic fibers. Gift of Bernard W. Ziobro, Gift of the Macedonian Arts Council, The Ronald Wixman/ Stephen Glaser Collection. There are five villages at the foot of Suva Gora Mountain where women wore this style of dress. The fitted sleeves with embroidery at the shoulder of the chemise are unique in the Macedonian repertoire. A chemise from the mid-nineteenth century would have the proportions of wool and silver-gilt thread embroidery reversed. The model wears a blouse, a chemise, a sleeveless coat of striped cotton with silver-gilt decoration on the fronts, a white cotton coat, *saya rhkae,* with vestigial sleeves covered in maroon pompoms, small and large aprons tied over a wool sash, a printed scarf tucked in at the waist, and a coin necklace called *gyerdan.* On the head is worn a *glaina* or braid holder that straps under the chin, a head scarf, and a pin, *igla.* Women wore *igla* in other parts of the country as well.

HALF SOCKS. *shutarke.* Suva Gora, c. 1900. A.2010.6.70V

Wool, length 11 ¹³⁄₁₆ in. (30 cm). Gift of Bernard W. Ziobro. Both half socks and socks were worn in this area.

SOCKS. *kalchini.* Suva Gora, c. 1900. A.2010.6.69V

Wool, length 16 ¹⁵⁄₁₆ in. (43 cm). Gift of Bernard W. Ziobro. The socks are gusseted on the side to make it easier to put them on.

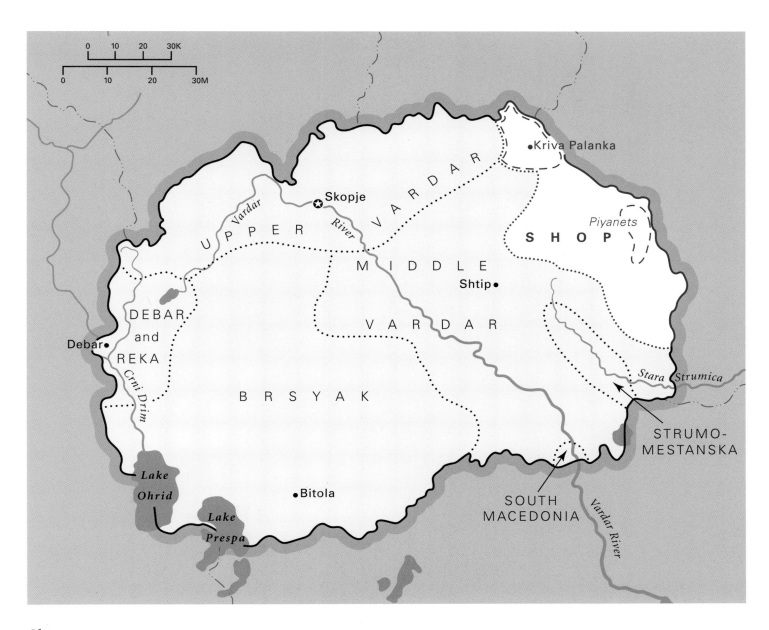

Shop

For the purpose of classifying dress, the Shop region describes a strip of land along the Bulgarian border from Kriva Palanka in the north to the municipality of Berovo in the south, a distance of approximately 65 miles. Other municipalities in the region are Makedonska Kamenica, Delchevo, Kochani, and Vinica. The ethnographic entity of Shop is much larger, encompassing most of the Middle Vardar sub-region. The population is primarily Macedonian with small numbers of Roma and others.

NEW BRIDE'S DRESS. Piyanets, Delchevo municipality, c. 1930

Wool, cotton, rayon, glass beads, metal, paper. Gift of Vladimir Janevski, Gift of Mike Zafirovski in memory of his parents. The differences between dress from western and eastern Macedonia are clearly visible in this ensemble. The chemise, made from blue-striped white cotton fabric, is not embroidered; a band of machine-made lace decorates the hem. The twill weave black wool coat, *saya,* the soberly striped apron and belt, *kutacha* and *poyas,* and the shoulder bag, *torba,* indicate that weaving was more important than embroidery in the area. Even the jewelry is gold instead of silver. The emphatic creases on the back of the coat and in the apron are deliberate, providing evidence of how the garments were stored: folded in chests in the villages.

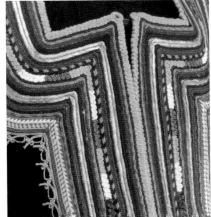

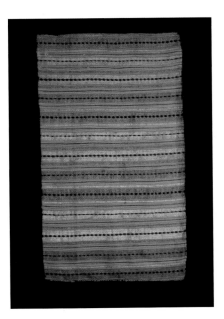

APRON. *telena dilyka.* Eastern Slavishte, Kriva Palanka municipality, c.1910.
A.2010.6.48

Wool, metallic thread, cotton, 28 ³⁄₈ x 16 ⁹⁄₁₆ in. (72 x 42 cm). Gift of Bernard W. Ziobro.

OVERCOAT. *shayak.* Eastern Slavishte, Kriva Palanka municipality, c.1910.
A.2010.6.54

Wool, metallic thread, cotton, silk, 41 x 32 ¼ in. (104 x 82 cm). Gift of Bernard W. Ziobro. When the coat from this area was made from home-produced, fulled wool, it was called *shayak*. The decoration on this example is the same as that on the *kazmir* garment described next.

NEW BRIDE'S DRESS. Eastern Slavishte, Kriva Palanka municipality, c. 1920

Cotton, wool, metallic thread, nylon, paper, metal, plastic. Gift of Bernard W. Ziobro, Gift of the Macedonian Arts Council. This dress consists of a dickey, a plain chemise embellished with lace on the sleeves and hem, a short-sleeved coat made from commercial wool fabric called *kazmir*, with fronts pinned back, an apron, a belt woven in the same technique as the apron, and a head scarf with flowers attached. Because it had to be purchased, *kazmir* had a higher value than the *shayak* produced at home. The municipality of Kriva Palanka borders on Serbia and Bulgaria; women on all sides of these borders wore a very similar style of dress.

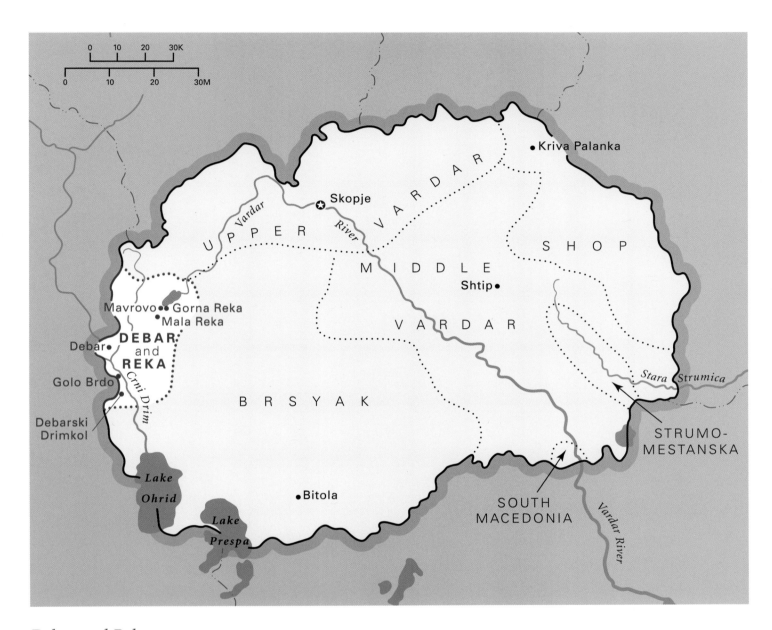

Debar and Reka

Debar and Reka is a small, mountainous region that lies on the Albanian border. It encompasses the rural municipalities of Mavrovo and Rostusha and Centar Zhupa, as well as the urban municipalities of Debar and Struga (the northern part only). When the border was redrawn after World War I, all the villages in the Golo Brdo area except Drenok became part of Albania. Historically and today it is a multiethnic, multireligious region with populations of both Orthodox and Muslim Macedonians, Albanians, Turks, and Roma. The terrain supports livestock, especially sheep, but not much farming. A tradition of migrating to find work elsewhere, known as *pechalbarstvo,* was common among the people of this region because it was hard to make a living here.

125

NEW BRIDE'S DRESS. Miyak, Mala Reka, c.1900

Cotton, wool, silk, metal, metallic thread, rayon. The Ronald Wixman/Stephen Glaser Collection, Gift of Bernard W. Ziobro, Museum Purchase. Mala Reka, on the western border, is the original land of the Miyaks, who migrated south and east from here beginning in the eighteenth century. Depicted here is the dress of a bride on the fourth and final day of the wedding festivities, when she went to the water fountain in the center of town to ritually wash the hands of the wedding party. The *tnoka* chemise worn the day before, during the church ceremony, has a particular type of embroidery called *pisani podvevci* (page 44) not seen on this chemise. Dressing began with a long-sleeved blouse, *mintan,* then the chemise, a vest, *elek,* and finally a heavy wool coat with vestigial sleeves, *klashenik.*

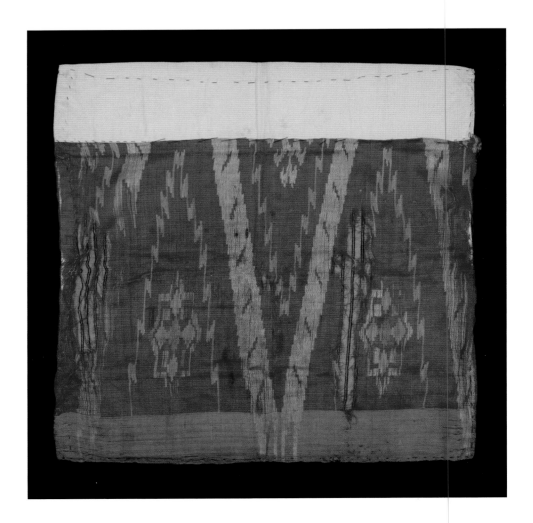

APRON. *stambolska futa.* Miyak, Mala Reka, c.1890

Silk, cotton, 23 ⅟₁₆ x 23 ¼ in. (58.5 x 59 cm). Gift of Bernard W. Ziobro. *Stambolska,* referencing the city of Istanbul, refers to the fact that the fabric of this apron was woven in Turkey. The motifs are woven with supplementary weft inserted against the red silk ground. Because of the apron's condition, the blue-striped cotton lining is visible. The apron is backed with heavy white cotton fabric that is visible at the top. The bride wore this apron only on the day after the wedding, not on the day of the church ceremony.

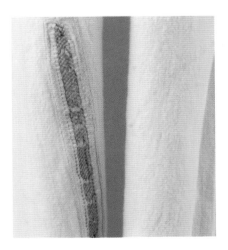

CHEMISE. *vodarska koshula.* Miyak, Mala Reka, c.1900. A.2010.6.33

Cotton, wool, metallic thread, length 46 ⅞ in. (119 cm). Gift of Bernard W. Ziobro. This Mala Reka chemise worn on the last day of the wedding ceremony, shows how the Miyak focused on sleeve embroidery. The detail clearly depicts the different stitches used.

APRON. *kivchena skutina.* Miyak, Mala Reka, c.1900. A.2008.7.49

Wool, 35 ⁷⁄₁₆ x 16 in. (90 x 40.5 cm). The Ronald Wixman/Stephen Glaser Collection. This is the apron the bride wore for the church wedding ceremony in Mala Reka. Woven in one long piece, it is folded over and tied so that the fringe falls as shown.

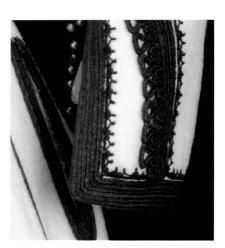

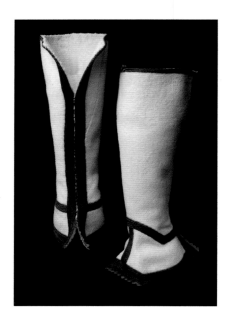

YOUNG MAN'S FESTIVAL DRESS. Miyak, c. 1900

Wool, cotton, leather. The Ronald Wixman / Stephen Glaser Collection, Gift of Bernard W. Ziobro, IFAF Collection. Miyak men wore very heavy wool garments all year round when attending festivals. A male tailor, *terzia,* constructed the garments. The decorative trim is called *gaitan.* A brown cotton shirt was worn under the pleated coat, *dolama.* Wool trousers, *bechvi,* a wool belt, *poyas,* a short wool jacket, *kepe,* a hat, *keche,* and leather shoes, *opinci* complete the outfit. Men of other ethnic and religious groups in Debar, some parts of the Brsyak region, and Albania wore the same style. The *dolama* was reserved for festival days, whereas the rest of the garments could be worn every day.

PUTTEES. *nazovtzi.* Miyak, Debar District, c. 1900. A.2010.6.136V

[Left] Wool, metal, cotton, length 16 ¹⁵⁄₁₆ in. (43 cm). Gift of Bernard W. Ziobro. A man wore *nazovtzi* when he had plain trousers without the decorative braid on the sides.

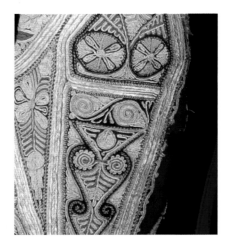

COAT. *dolama*. Gorna Reka, c. 1890. FA.2008.23.13

Wool, cotton, silk, metallic thread, coral, length 41⅜ in. (105 cm). IFAF Collection. This woman's coat has the same name as the man's coat above and is constructed in the same way. The bodice is loosely sewn to the skirt, which is made up of 35 tapered pieces. Each seam is covered with braid. The Miyak man's *dolama* skirt is made from 20 pieces with narrow braid sewn over each seam. The bodice and sleeves of this coat are covered with couched designs and silver-gilt braid. Each button has a tiny coral bead on the top.

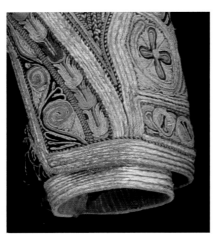

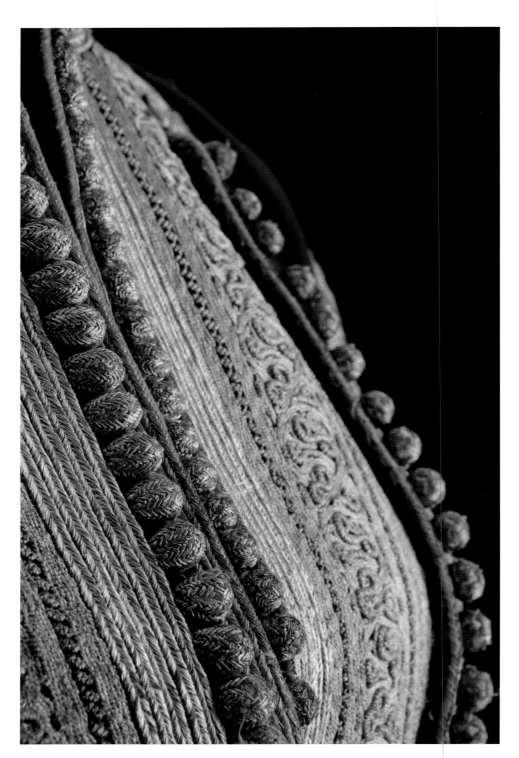

WEDDING DRESS. Gorna Reka, c.1900

[Details of Following Spread] Cotton, wool, metallic thread, metallic tape, silk, metal, rayon, coral, glass beads. IFAF Collection, Gift of Mike Zafirovski in memory of his parents, Gift of Mr. and Mrs. William F. Hennessey. The bride's dress in Gorna Reka differed from that of Miyak neighbors in Mala Reka. The pleated and embroidered *dolama* for women is unique to this area. The small ornament at the throat made from yarns and coins is called *kiska;* the same word refers to fringe, a bouquet, and also a sprig of a plant.[2] Women in Gorna Reka also wore a red print scarf around the hips, *shamiya.* But the styles shared some features, too, including the long-sleeved blouse, the vest with gold embroidery and buttons worn under the coat, and the use of purchased scarves around the waist. The jewelry usually worn by a bride is missing. [2] Vesna Mladenovic, "Threads of Life: Red Fringes in Macedonian Dress" in *Folk Dress in Europe and Anatolia: Beliefs about Protection and Fertility,* ed. L. Welters (Oxford: Berg, 1999).

BELT. *kolan.* Gorna Reka, Mavrovsko Pole and Gorni Polog, c. 1910. FA.1969.43.11

[Lower image] Leather, glass beads, metal, cotton, wire, wool, 33 7/16 x 4 3/4 in. (85 x 12 cm). IFAF Collection. The coins on this belt are from the Ottoman Empire, dated 1223 in the Hijiri calendar, 1808 by the Gregorian; Serbia, dated 1904 and 1915; and the Austrian Empire, dated 1765 and 1785. A bride or recently married woman would have worn the belt.

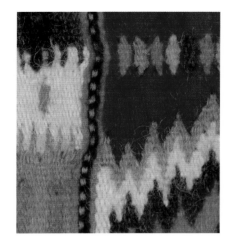

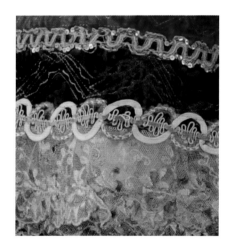

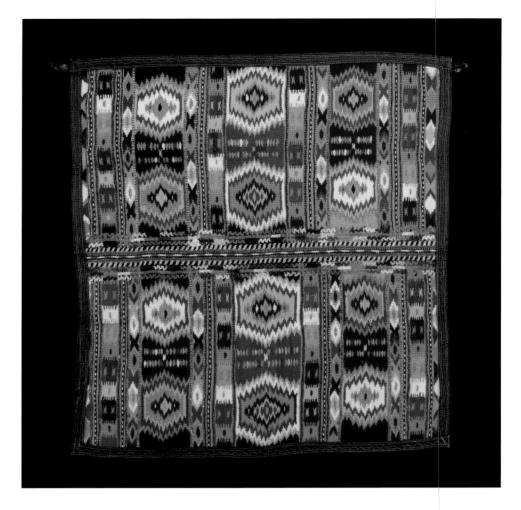

APRON. *lepa bovcha.* Debarsko Pole, c. 1920. A.2010.6.43

Wool, cotton, 28⅜ x 26 in. (72 x 66 cm). Gift of Bernard W. Ziobro. *Lepa,* from the root word *lep,* means "beautiful," thus the name of this item is "beautiful apron." It was woven in one piece, the warp at a 90° angle to how it is worn, and cut to make two pieces that were joined with multicolored needlework. There is a little embroidery on either side of the center seam.

WEDDING DRESS. Debarsko Pole, c. 1920

Cotton, wool, silk, rayon, metal, plastic. Gift of Bernard W. Ziobro, Gift of the Macedonian Arts Council. The Debarsko Pole bridal dress changed significantly from the late nineteenth to the early twentieth century. Whereas the chemise worn by the mannequin is a tube of fabric open on both ends and tied at the waist, the older chemise had embroidered sleeves, a front opening, and white needlework on the hem. Unique in Macedonia, the sleeve embroidery was worked in drawn-thread netting. Here, detachable sleeves sewn from strips of velvet trimmed with lace and tapes have replaced the older sleeves. The other change was from a red to light red range of colors to the bright pink seen here. Craftsmen made the two vests, *elek* and *pregrlak,* and the short-sleeved coat, *lepo zobanche,* from home-produced and purchased fabrics.

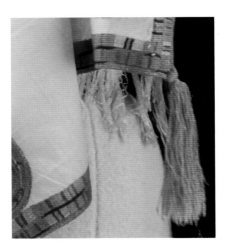

CAP. *kapa.* Debarsko Pole, c.1920. A.2010.6.46

Silk, cotton, height 3 ¹⁵⁄₁₆ in. (10 cm). Gift of Bernard W. Ziobro. Nearly invisible when worn, the cap creates the foundation for the head scarf. Embroidery with cord is worked over velvet cloth. The cap incorporates some stiffening material and is lined with cotton. It was made by a craftsman.

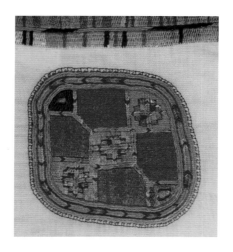

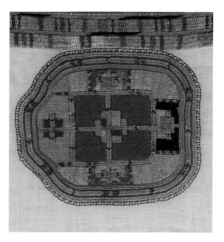

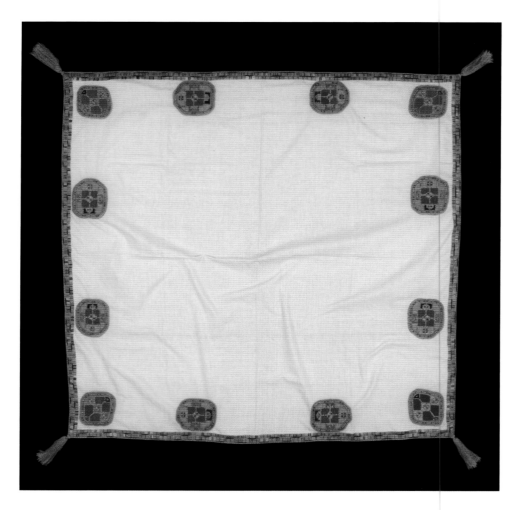

HEAD CLOTH. *darpna.* Debarsko Pole, c. 1920. A.2010.6.47

Cotton, silk, 41 ⁵⁄₁₆ x 41 ⁵⁄₁₆ in. (105 x 105 cm). Gift of Bernard W. Ziobro. This bridal head cloth with twelve *vetki* or oval motifs uses yellow silk embroidery thread in place of the silver-gilt thread seen in older pieces.

HEAD CLOTH. *darpna.* Debarsko Pole, c. 1860. A.1949.1.93

Cotton, silk, 39 ¾ x 40 ¾ in. (101 x 103.5 cm). Gift of Mrs. Dwight B. Heard. Two older *darpni* in the collection show the earlier color scheme, as well as sixteen *vetki* (oval motifs) with different designs. This one has four of the same motif in the corners and four of a different motif in the middle of each side. These middle *vetki* are each flanked by two of an entirely different motif. Women wore head cloths with diverse motifs at each life stage.

HEAD CLOTH. *darpna klabodanliya.* Debarsko Pole, c. 1870. A.1995.93.784

Cotton, silk, metallic thread, 32 x 35 in. (81.3 x 88.9 cm). Gift of Lloyd E. Cotsen and the Neutrogena Corporation. This example incorporates silver-gilt thread, *klabodan,* and was probably meant for a bride. It displays two different *vetki.*

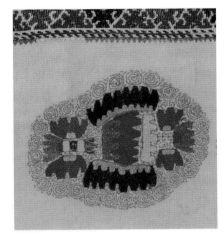

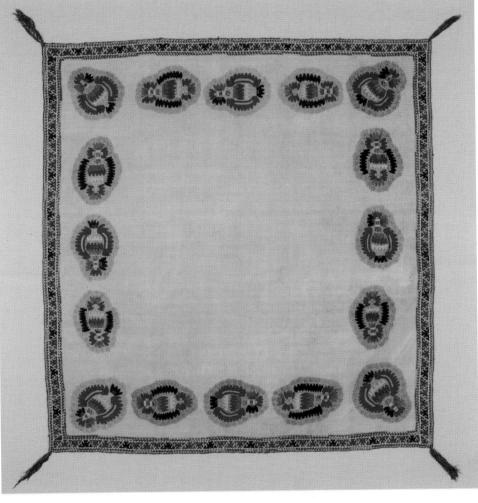

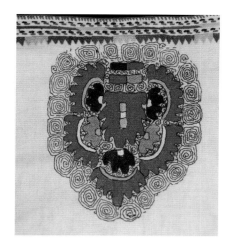

HEAD CLOTH. *darpna.* Debarsko Pole, c. 1860. A.1949.1.93

NEW BRIDE'S DRESS. Debarski Drimkol, c. 1910

Cotton, wool, metallic thread, metal, glass beads. The Ronald Wixman/Stephen Glaser Collection, IFAF Collection, Gift of Mr. and Mrs. William F. Hennessey. A newly married woman wore this ensemble on the fourth day of the wedding ceremony, when she went to the well for the ritual handwashing. The garment that distinguishes this from the wedding day ensemble is the chemise, *so sedum lozi* "with seven vines." From the rear, the seven vines can be seen on the sleeve. An embroidered dickey is worn over the chemise. On top of that is a gold-embellished sleeveless jacket, *klashenik,* several belts to fill out the waist, the apron, *skutina,* a red print hip scarf covered in sequins, another red scarf tucked into the waist, a short vest, *kusale,* and a head scarf, *korpa.* Two pieces of the vest fringe are tied around the scarf fringe to hold it in place. A bride would have worn silver jewelry on the wedding day.

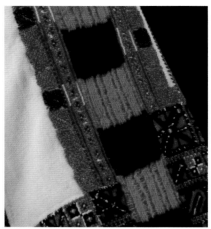

NEW BRIDE'S DRESS. Debarski Drimkol, c. 1910

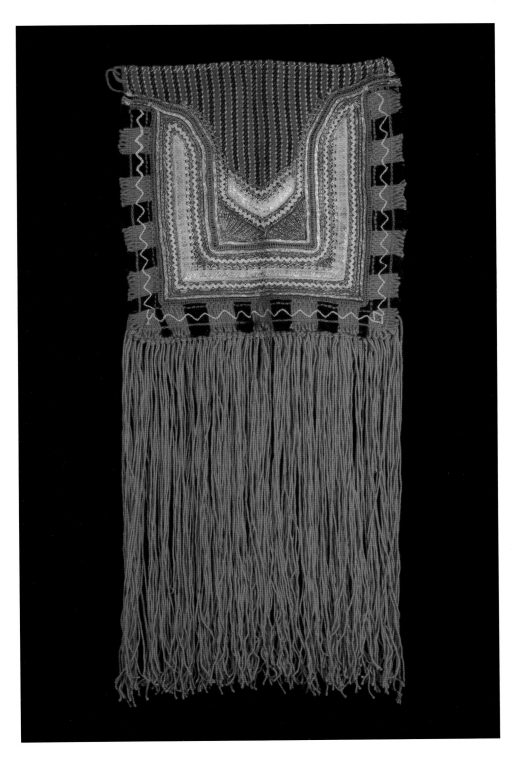

APRON. *skutina*. Debarski Drimkol, c.1890. A.2009.15.47

Wool, cotton, metallic thread, 33⅟₁₆ x 13⁹⁄₁₆ in. (84 x 34.5 cm). The Ronald Wixman/ Stephen Glaser Collection. This small apron, worn by a bride (and the mannequin) and nearly obscured by all that is worn on top of it, is made of home-woven wool plaid decorated with metallic threads and tapes. The long fringe here and on the head scarf protected a bride during a most vulnerable period.

SOCKS. *kolchini.* Debarski Drimkol, c. 1890. A.2009.15.50v

Wool, length 19 ¹¹⁄₁₆ in. (50 cm). The Ronald Wixman/Stephen Glaser Collection. Hand-knit socks were an important aspect of dress for everyone in Macedonia. Women's socks were shorter than men's.

SOCKS. *kolchini.* Golo Brdo, c. 1900. A.2008.7.63

Wool, length 20½ in. (53 cm). The Ronald Wixman/Stephen Glaser Collection.

WEDDING DRESS. Golo Brdo, c.1900

Cotton, wool, metallic thread, metal, glass beads. Gift of Bernard W. Ziobro, Gift of Mike Zafirovski in memory of his parents, The Ronald Wixman/Stephen Glaser Collection, IFAF Collection. The village of Drenok, on the Macedonian side of Golo Brdo, is about 21 miles south of Debar. Brides there and in the villages now in Albania wore this ensemble. The close relationship of this outfit to the dress of Debarski Drimkol is clear, with strong similarities as well as distinct differences. The stitches used for the embroidery on the sleeves and the head scarf create a different texture, flatter and smoother. The layout of the sleeve is similar—the same band of *poplitz* runs from wrist to shoulder—but the motifs used are entirely different. Two sets of fringe on the apron and very long fringe on each end of the belt, as well as long red tassels attached to the waist scarf, *naniz,* contribute to the visual and aural impression that the bride would have made. The swishing of fringe was associated with the movement of waves in water and linked to the vitality of nature.[3] Ibid

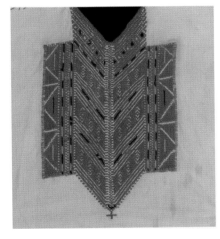

WEDDING DRESS. Golo Brdo, c.1900

APRON. *bokchenitsa.* Golo Brdo, c.1900. A.2010.6.23

Wool, cotton, metallic thread, 27 9⁄16 x 9 15⁄16 in. (70 x 25 cm). Gift of Bernard W. Ziobro. The Golo Brdo wedding apron starts with a base fabric of orange-and blue-striped twill, the same as the apron from Debarski Drimkol. The front is then covered with highly twisted cords that hang down on each side to make additional fringe. Silver-gilt-wrapped thread and ribbon decoration are attached.

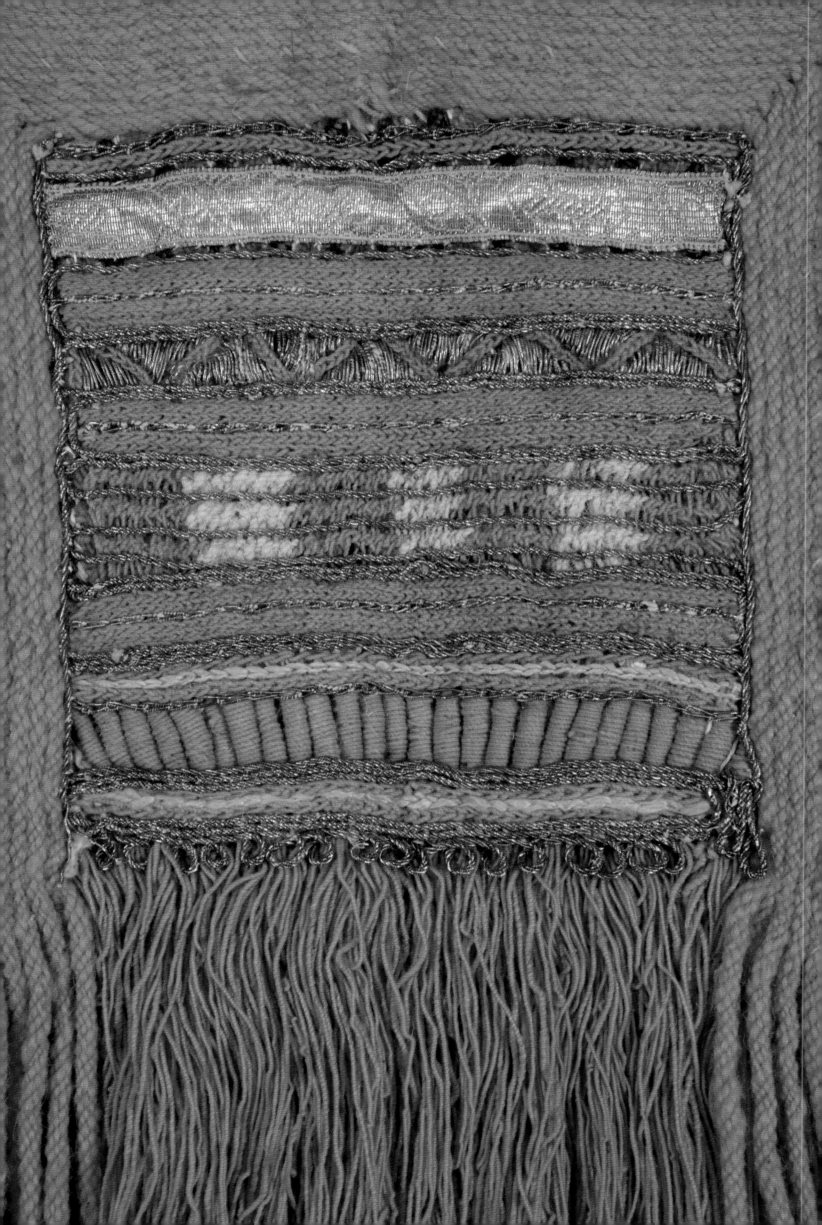

WEDDING CHEMISE. *koshula tnoka.* Golo Brdo, c.1890. A.2008.7.56

Cotton, wool, length 54 ¾ in. (139 cm). The Ronald Wixman/Stephen Glaser Collection. Two large blue and red eight-pointed stars were always embroidered on the sleeve of a wedding chemise.

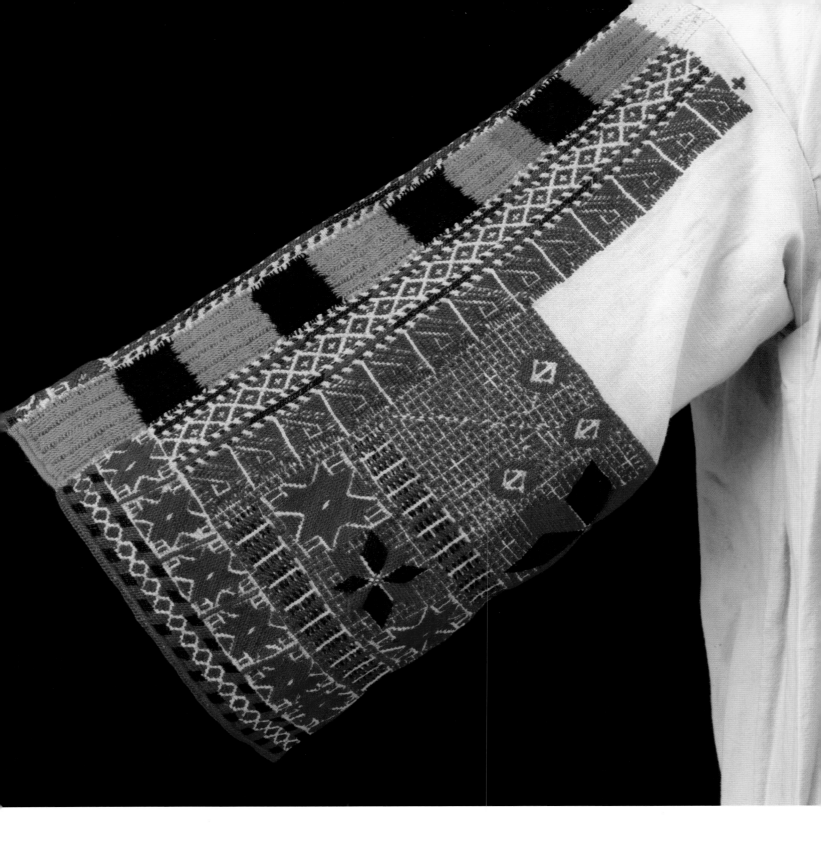

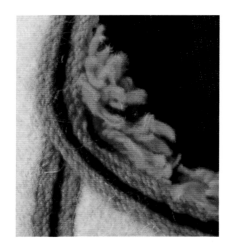

VEST. *kusale.* Golo Brdo, c. 1890. A.2008.7.57

Wool, 16⅛ x 12³⁄₁₆ in. (41 x 31 cm). The Ronald Wixman/Stephen Glaser Collection. Older women wore the *kusale* as everyday dress.

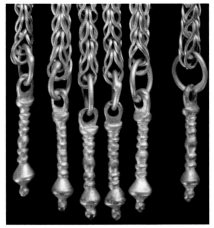

EARRINGS. *ushnitsi*. Debarsko Pole, c. 1880. A.1955.1.394 SC

Metal, glass, carnelian, 8 ⁷⁄₁₆ x 2 ³⁄₁₆ in. (21.5 x 5.5 cm). Gift of Florence Dibell Bartlett. A fine chain attached to each earring and worn over the head supported their weight in the ears.

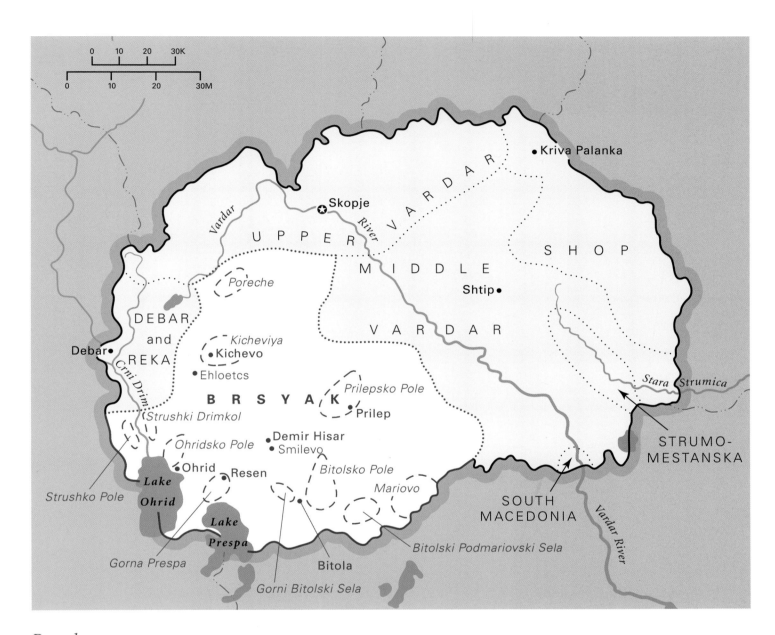

Brsyak

The Brsyak region covers nearly half of the country of Macedonia, from west of the Vardar River to the Greek and Albanian borders. Varied topography, from high mountains to the extensive Pelagonia Valley, creates different environmental conditions and affects how people make their livelihood. The urban centers of Bitola and Prilep were cosmopolitan in their population, whereas the villages were usually homogenous. The rural people were primarily Macedonian with small numbers of other ethnicities.

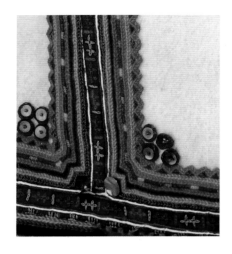

WEDDING DRESS. Gorni Bitolski Sela, c.1900

Wool, cotton, metal, metallic thread, glass beads. The Ronald Wixman/Stephen Glaser Collection, Gift of Bernard W. Ziobro, IFAF Collection. The villages in this area are known as the Upper Villages of Bitola. Among the Brsyak villages there were many similarities in dress but with locally significant details. The similarities include the use of a long black wool belt that was wrapped around the waist to create a straighter silhouette and thus better presentation of the apron. The belt, called *poyas,* was made of braided wool. The braids were used singly in some places or were sewn together to make a wider belt as here. The color orange replaced the madder red shades of the earlier nineteenth century. Another common feature was the embroidered appliqué on the front of the sleeveless wool *shayak* (overcoat). These decorations were usually done on a base of red cotton cloth. The *skopetz* or coin chain fastened at the waist is particular to the Brsyak as well.

DICKEY. *grlo.* Gorni Bitolski Sela, c. 1920. A.2008.7.2

Cotton, 20 ½ x 17 ¹¹⁄₁₆ in. (52 x 45 cm). The Ronald Wixman/Stephen Glaser Collection. The embroidered *grlo* kept a woman's chest covered and provided another canvas for stitching.

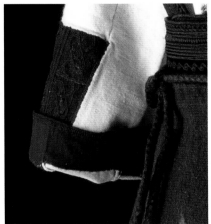

WEDDING DRESS. Gorni Bitolski Sela, c. 1950

[Details of Following Spread] Cotton, wool, silk, glass beads, metal, polyester. The Ronald Wixman/Stephen Glaser Collection. In the early years of the twentieth century the bridal dress of some of the villages around Bitola went from multicolored to black embroidery. It is said the change occurred because of the sorrow and poverty caused by the political and economic upheaval of the Balkan Wars and World War I and the concurrent departure of many men to seek work in America.[4] Other changes in the chemise include shorter but wider back embroidery, *boyovi,* and the addition of a strip of crocheted lace along the bottom. A tailor would have decorated the wool jacket with black braid, and the garment is less generous than the older one above. The entire wedding ensemble is far simpler than that worn earlier. [4] Penka Matovska, *From Macedonian Treasury* (Bitola: Združenie Makedonska Riznica, 1999).

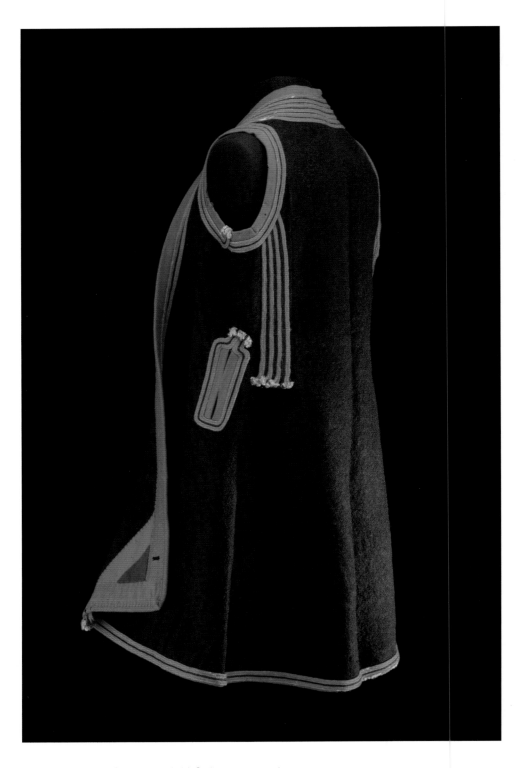

COAT. *gornik.* Gorni Bitolski Sela, c. 1900. A.2009.15.18

Wool, 41 5/16 x 32 11/16 in. (108 x 83 cm). The Ronald Wixman/Steven Glaser Collection. Worn by a married woman for Sunday best, this plain coat contrasts with the bridal *shayak* on the mannequin on page 166.

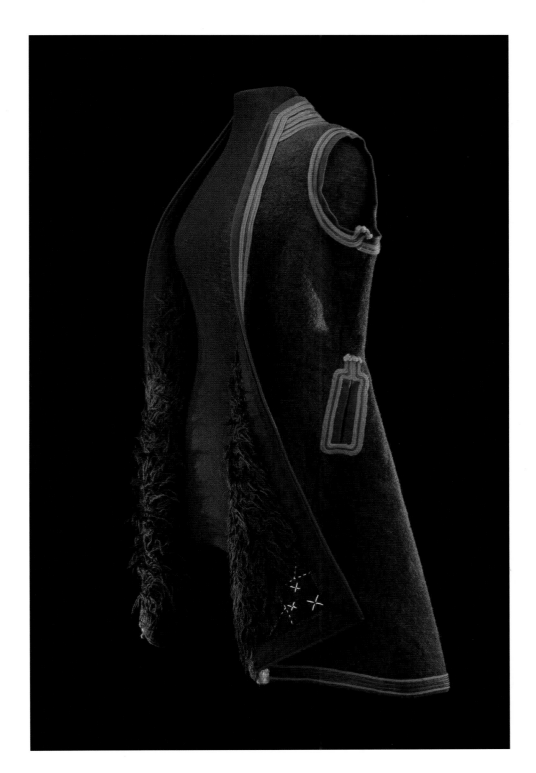

COAT. *resachka.* Gorni Bitolski Sela, c. 1900. A.2009.15.26

Wool, 38 ³⁄₁₆ x 29 ½ in. (97 x 75 cm). The Ronald Wixman/Steven Glaser Collection.
When the black wool outer garment is covered with fringe on the inside, it's called
resachka and would have been worn by a young married woman in the winter.

CHEMISE. *alska koshula*. Gorni Bitolski Sela, c. 1880. A.2009.15.14

Cotton, wool, length 50 ¹³/₁₆ in. (129 cm). The Ronald Wixman/Stephen Glaser Collection. The sleeves were unfortunately cut but the embroidery is extraordinary on this red chemise. The colors used are typical of the older work using madder.

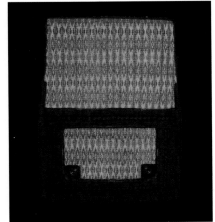

APRON. *pregach.* Bitolsko Pole, c. 1920. A.2009.15.23

Wool, cotton, 24 x 17 15/16 in. (61 x 45.5 cm). The Ronald Wixman/Stephen Glaser Collection. Brides in the villages located on the Pelagonia Plain typically wore this style of wedding apron. It is a combination of cloth woven at home in tapestry technique and applied trim of velveteen and different types of braid.

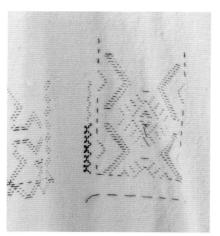

CHEMISE. *koshula*. Bitolsko-Prilepsko Pole, c. 1960. FA.1972.26.3a

Cotton, wool, glass beads, sequins, length 46 7/16 in. (118 cm). IFAF Collection. This is perhaps the last version made of a Bitola chemise. The sleeves were cut short and finished with blue binding. The over-embroidery on the sleeves and the work on the bottom of the dress was done quickly with thick threads. In a style typical of the latest pieces, a lot of beads were used to outline the circular motifs on the hem. The pattern outlines on the front are called *zaorok*.

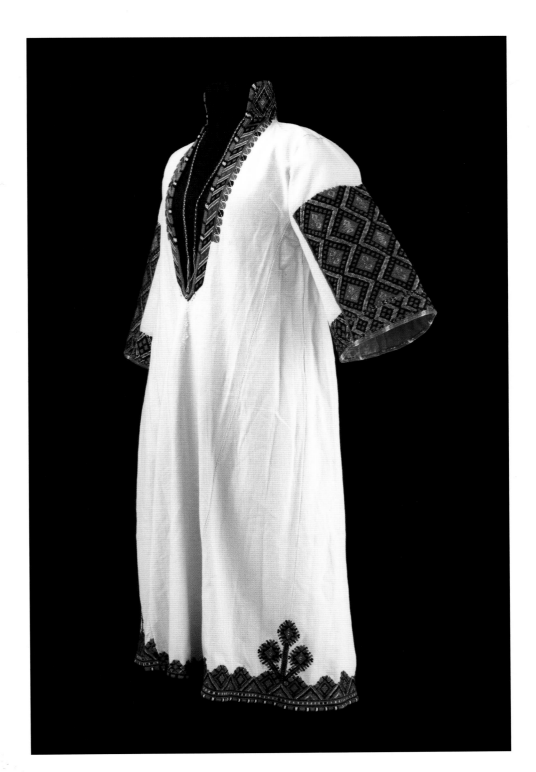

CHEMISE. *grabena koshula.* Bitolsko Pole, c.1900. A.2010.6.106

Cotton, wool, length 46 1/16 in. (117 cm). Gift of Bernard W. Ziobro. The use of the *granka* or branched motif on the side seam indicates that a married woman would have worn this chemise, which is embroidered entirely in the *grabena* or horizontal straight stitch. This stitch creates more dimension than the flatter, slanted Slav stitch.

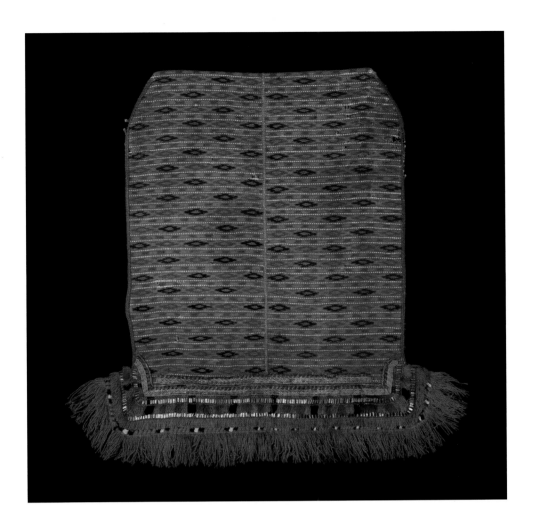

APRON. *chultar.* Bitolsko Pole, c.1880. A.1978.2.5

Wool, brass, metallic thread, 33 ¹⁄₁₆ x 32 ⁵⁄₁₆ in. (84 x 82 cm). Gift of Mrs. Frank Hibben. The *chultar* is another bridal apron. A bride would have worn it underneath another apron on her wedding day. Although very similar to the *chultar* from Prilep, this one was woven in two pieces and joined vertically. The Prilep *chultar* was woven in one piece.

NEW BRIDE'S DRESS. Bitolski Podmariovski Sela, c. 1910

[Details of Following Spread] Cotton, wool, glass beads, metal coins, metal sequins, silk. The Ronald Wixman/Stephen Glaser Collection, Gift of Bernard W. Ziobro. Dress from this area—between the Pelagonia Plain villages and the Mariovo villages on a high plateau—shows elements of both places. The chemise and apron are similar to those of the lower villages, while the use of the *ubrus* on the head and fringes on the outer *klashenik* are similar to Mariovo. On the shoulders is pinned a black woolen braid, *prtzle*, that hangs below the fringe of the *ubrus*. The recently married woman would dress this way on Sundays, festive occasions, and weddings for the first year after the wedding or until she gave birth. Other elements of the outfit include the *skopetz* coin jewelry and the dickey, *grlo,* ornamented with embroidery, sequins, and beads.

CHEMISE. *krstatna koshula.* Bitolski Podmariovski Sela, c. 1900. A.2008.7.15

Cotton, wool, glass beads, metal coins, length 49 ⅝ in. (126 cm). The Ronald Wixman/ Stephen Glaser Collection. Shown on the new bride mannequin, this chemise is named *krstatna* for the many different cross motifs on the sleeves and the bottom. A single row of black and white glass beads decorates the bottom of the sleeve.

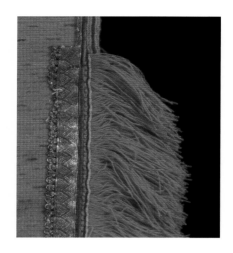

APRON. *pregach.* Mariovo, c. 1900. A.2008.7.31

Wool, metal, metallic thread, 29 ½ x 23 ¹³⁄₁₆ in. (75 x 60.5 cm). The Ronald Wixman/ Stephen Glaser Collection.

WEDDING DRESS. Mariovo, c. 1900

[Details of Following Spread] Cotton, wool, metal, metallic thread, glass beads. The Ronald Wixman/Stephen Glaser Collection, Gift of Bernard W. Ziobro. The wedding ensemble from Mariovo, the region encompassing many villages at high elevation in the Nidzhe and Selechki Mountains, is the heaviest in all Macedonia. The only colors used were shades of red, black, yellow, and white. The people living there were very isolated and self-sufficient; their customs and traditions, including dress and religious practices, took a different path from that of other Brsyak people lower down the mountains.[5] The amount and placement of fringe on the outer garments, the apron, and the detached sleevelets, *rakavchinya vezeni,* all worn by the bride, are unique. Garments and jewelry on this mannequin include a dickey, chemise, apron, two belts, sleevelets, sleeveless cotton coat, *sagiya,* sleeveless wool coat, *gornenik,* two belt buckles, two strings of coin jewelry on the apron, one string of coin jewelry at the neck, two disks attached to the front of the wool coat, two head scarves with pompoms, *tulben,* one scarf tucked into the apron, and a head cloth, *ubrus.* On the wedding day, the *ubrus* was pulled down to cover the bride's eyes and her head was crowned with a large wreath of flowers and greenery. [5] Ibid., 45

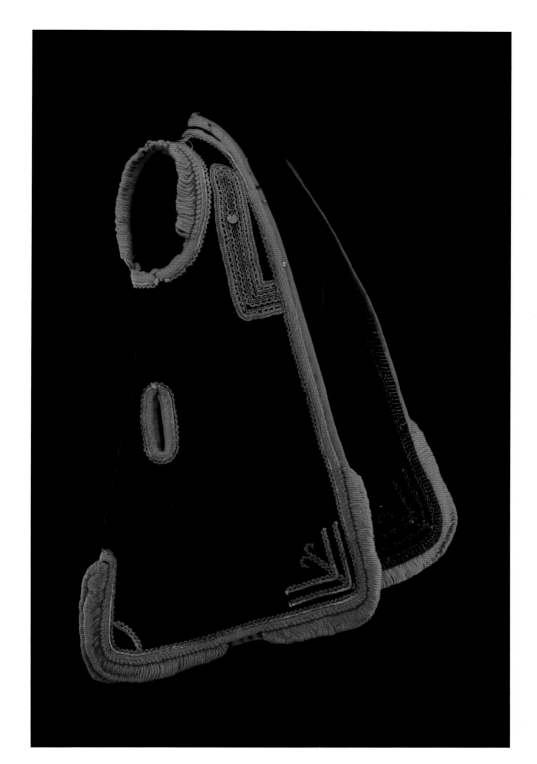

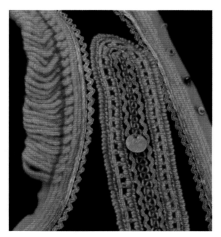

OVERCOAT. *guna.* Mariovo, c.1900. A.2008.7.17

Wool, metallic thread, metal, glass beads, 32 ⁵⁄₁₆ x 26 ⁹⁄₁₆ in. (82 x 67.5 cm). The Ronald
Wixman/Stephen Glaser Collection. Married women wore the black *guna* for Sunday
best.

OVERCOAT. *gornenik.* Mariovo, c.1900. A.2008.7.30

[Left] Wool, cotton, metallic thread, metal, 32¼ x 29⅛ in. (82 x 74 cm). The Ronald
Wixman/Stephen Glaser Collection. This is another example of the bridal *gornenik*
of Mariovo. Although this one is different from the one on the mannequin, the black
fringe on both identifies them as bridal. A newly married woman wore the *gornenik*
on feast days and special occasions for several years after her wedding.

SOCKS. *chorabi.* Mariovo, c. 1900. A.2008.7.35V

Wool, length 19 ¹¹⁄₁₆ in. (50 cm). The Ronald Wixman/Stephen Glaser Collection.

SOCKS. *chorabi.* Mariovo, c. 1900. A.2010.6.125v

Wool, length 21 ¼ in. (54 cm). Gift of Bernard W. Ziobro. Socks from Mariovo show
the continued use of a limited color palette.

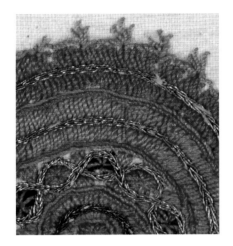

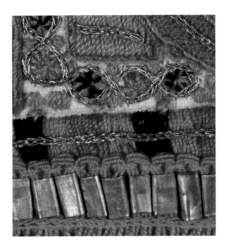

SLEEVELETS. c. 1900
[Image directly above]

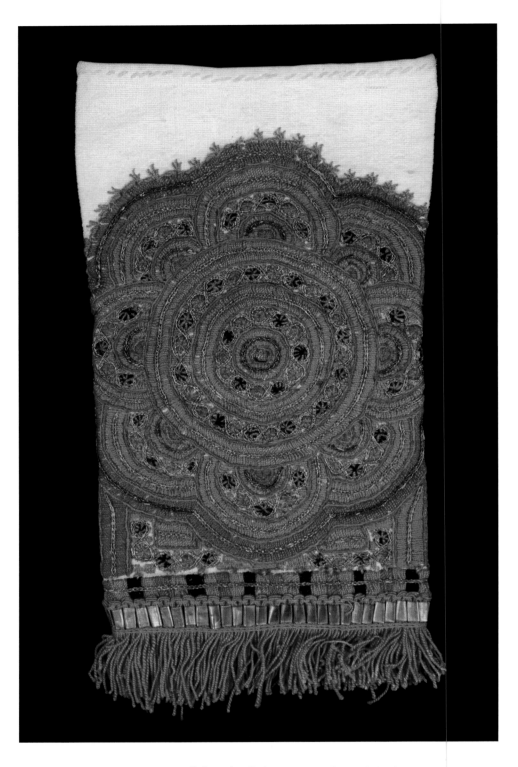

SLEEVELETS. *rakavchinya.* Prilepsko Pole, c. 1880. A.1978.2.12

Cotton, wool, metal, metallic thread, length 11½ in. (29.5 cm). Gift of Mrs. Frank Hibben. Looked at side by side, these two sleeves from different time periods show a common design executed with slightly different materials. The black and white beads on the later piece mimic the black embroidery on the earlier piece. Both are masterfully embroidered.

NEW BRIDE'S DRESS. Prilepsko Pole, c. 1900

[Details of Following Spread] Cotton, wool, metal, metallic thread, glass beads, bast fiber. The Ronald Wixman/Stephen Glaser Collection, Gift of Bernard W. Ziobro, Gift of Mr. and Mrs. William F. Hennessey. Along with the fifteen items already on this mannequin, including three long black belts, a bride would also have worn another apron, a pair of short knitted wristlets, and two other pieces of head gear at her wedding. Coins decorate the neckpiece, called *gyerdan,* several jewelry chains, and two belts visible from the back. The city of Prilep is about 30 miles north-northeast of Bitola, but the similarities between wedding clothing from these two Brsyak areas are unmistakable.

SOCKS. *chorabi*. Prilepsko Pole, c. 1890. A.2009.15.9v

Wool, length 18 ⅞ in. (48 cm). The Ronald Wixman/Stephen Glaser Collection. *Chorabi, kolchini, kalchini,* and *perpoci* are all terms used by different groups in Macedonia for socks.

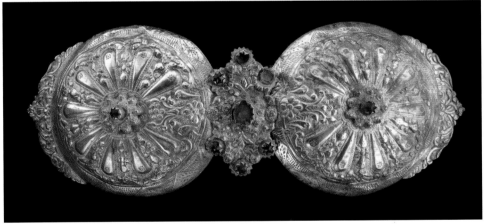

BUCKLE. *kubele pafta*. Prilepsko Pole, c.1900. A.2010.6.86V

Metal, length 11 ¹³⁄₁₆ in. (30 cm). Gift of Bernard W. Ziobro.

BUCKLE. *pafta*. Prilepsko Pole, c.1900. A.2009.15.11V

Metal, glass, length 14 in. (36 cm). The Ronald Wixman/Stephen Glaser Collection.

APRON. *skutinik.* Kicheviya, c. 1920. A.2009.15.42

Wool, cotton, 27 9/16 x 15 15/16 in. (70 x 43 cm). The Ronald Wixman/Stephen Glaser Collection. This strikingly modern apron is bound on three edges with red cotton fabric.

WEDDING DRESS. Kicheviya, c. 1920

Cotton, wool, metal, metallic thread, silk, glass beads. The Ronald Wixman/Stephen Glaser Collection. The bride was led from her house to the church covered with a hood fashioned from a Miyak man's wide wool sash; the groom's family provided the sash for this purpose. She wore this hood during the church service. The best man finally removed it when she arrived at the groom's house. This was customary in Kicheviya, Zheleznik, and Debarsko Pole. Sometimes a length of red cotton fabric was sewn into a hood, replacing the woven sash. The use of a man's sash provided by the groom's family symbolized the joining of the bride to the groom.[6] G. Zdravev, *Macedonian Folk Costumes* (Skopje: Matica Makedonska, 2005), 259.

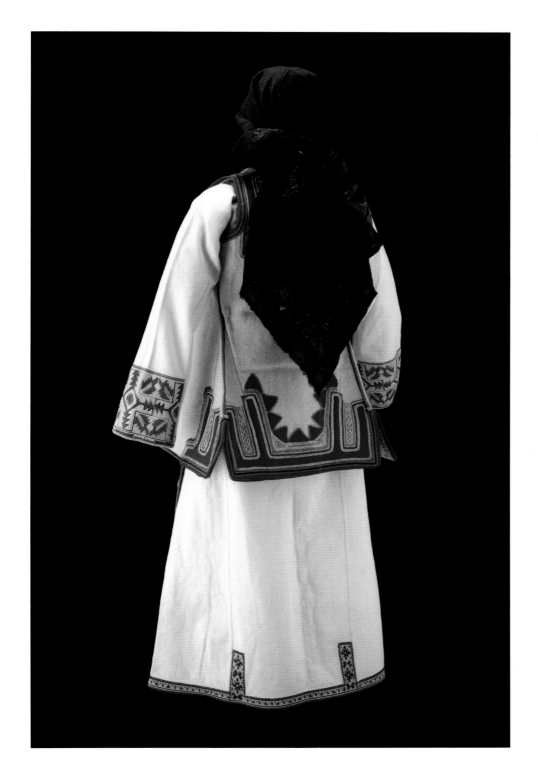

WEDDING DRESS. Kicheviya, c. 1920

Cotton, wool, metal, metallic thread, silk, glass beads. The Ronald Wixman/Stephen Glaser Collection. The ensemble worn by Brsyak women in this part of the region is simpler than that worn in Bitola or Prilep; they wore far fewer garments. Lighter colors and less ornamentation overall were typical. The bride wore a more fitted chemise and two white wool sleeveless jackets. The deliberately offset stripes of the apron, the black braid belts visible underneath, and the dangling chain of coins draw the attention immediately to the reproductive area of the body.

DICKEY. *grlo.* Kicheviya, c. 1910. A.2008.7.1

Cotton, glass beads, 17 ½ x 15 ⅜ in. (44.5 x 39 cm). The Ronald Wixman/Stephen Glaser Collection. Some styles of dickeys were more regional than village specific; this one could have been worn in other villages in the Brsyak region as well.

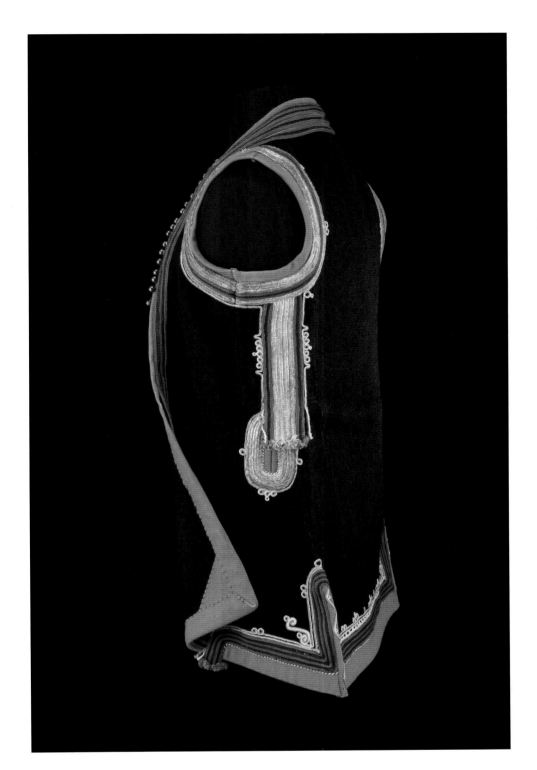
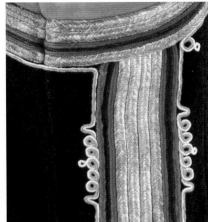

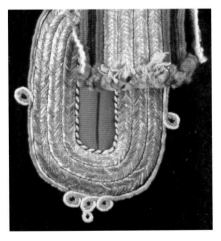

JACKET. *kyurdiya.* Kicheviya, c.1920. A.2009.15.43

Wool, cotton, metallic thread, metal, 29 ¹⁵⁄₁₆ x 21 ⅝ in. (76 x 55 cm). The Ronald Wixman/Stephen Glaser Collection. Made from fulled black wool, this jacket was worn by a bride on the day after her wedding, as well as on holiday and festive occasions. Small brass buttons decorate both upper front edges.

CHEMISE. *alska koshula.* Kicheviya, c. 1920. A.2009.15.40

Cotton, wool, length 49 3/16 in. (125 cm). The Ronald Wixman / Stephen Glaser Collection. The slimmer silhouette of the Kicheviya chemise is evident when seen alone. Although the placement of the embroidery on the sleeve, hem, and neck is the same all over the region, the amount of embroidery varies in different places and times, as well as for different uses.

HEAD CLOTH. *ubrus.* Poreche, c. 1890. A.2011.8.1

Cotton, wool, metallic thread, silk, 30 5/8 x 9 1/2 in. (77 x 24 cm). Gift of Sharon Sharpe. The Poreche *ubrus* is a spectacular example of the embroiderer's art; it is the same front and back. A bride wore it during the wedding ceremony, draped over another head piece called a *sokay* and covered with a cloth that obscured her face. All these elements can be seen in a remarkable series of photographs taken by the ethnographer Joseph Obrebski in 1932–33.[7] Tanas Vrashinovski, ed. *Joseph Obrebski: Macedonian Poreche 1932–1933* (Prilep and Skopje: Institute for Slavonic Culture and Matica, 2003).

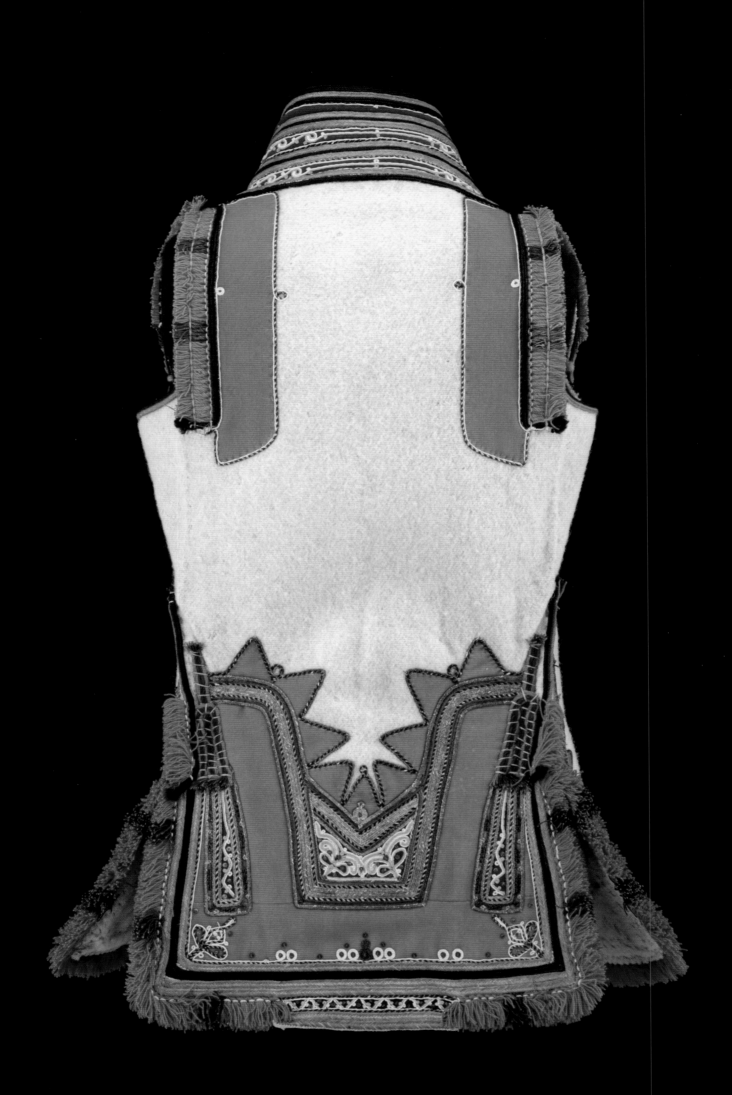

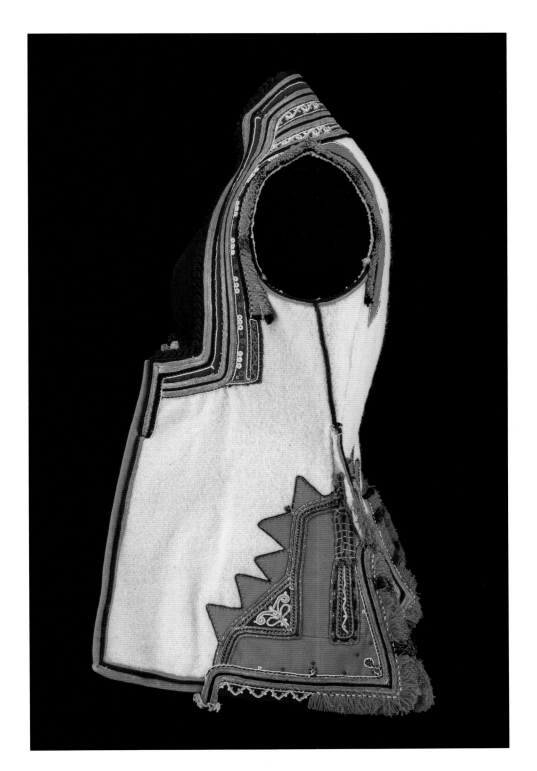
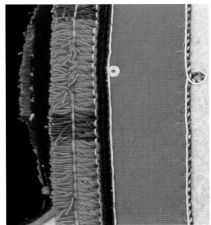
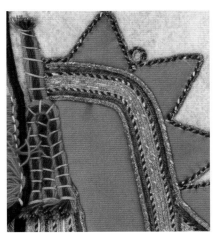

JACKET. *klashenik.* Poreche, c. 1890. A.1978.2.2

Wool, cotton, metallic thread, silk, metal, 29⅛ x 14⅛ in. (74 x 36 cm). Gift of Mrs. Frank Hibben. Poreche is an isolated mountain region north of the city of Kichevo and across the mountains from Gostivar. The amount of silver and decoration on this *klashenik* indicate it was a wedding garment. Photos taken in 1932–33 in the villages of Poreche show women at work wearing the asymmetrical striped apron of Kicheviya and a black or white, sparsely decorated *klashenik*, the color depending on age.

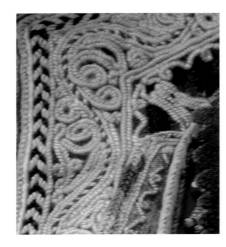

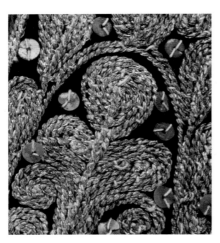

WEDDING DRESS. Miyak, Smilevo, Demir Hisar municipality, c. 1900

[Details of Following Spread] Wool, cotton, silk, metallic thread, metal, glass beads, plastic. The Ronald Wixman/Stephen Glaser Collection, IFAF Collection, Gift of the Macedonian Arts Council. Demir Hisar is north-northwest of Bitola and southeast of the Miyak homeland. The layers of garments and the color harmony seen in all the Miyak outfits is evident here as well. The four upper garments start with the *mintan* or long-sleeved velvet blouse, then the wedding chemise, *pisa koshula,* with *pisani podvevchi* motifs (see page 44), an *elek* or vest with purple velvet front, and finally a wool coat with vestigial sleeves. A long sash, *prepashka,* wrapped so the fringe falls over the hips, and an apron, *kivchena skutina,* with two tiers of fringe surrounds the middle of the body. The red *glaina sokay* fitted to the head with a seam, and a cord under the chin hangs down the back. A sheer *darpna* with gold work covers that and holds an *igla,* a type of head jewelry. Under the *pafta* the *krst shamiya* covers the top of the apron.

WEDDING DRESS. Miyak, Smilevo, Demir Hisar municipality, c. 1900

SOCKS. *chorabi.* Miyak, Smilevo, Demir Hisar municipality, c.1900. A.2008.7.8v

Wool, length 20 ¹⁄₁₆ in. (51 cm). The Ronald Wixman/Stephen Glaser Collection.

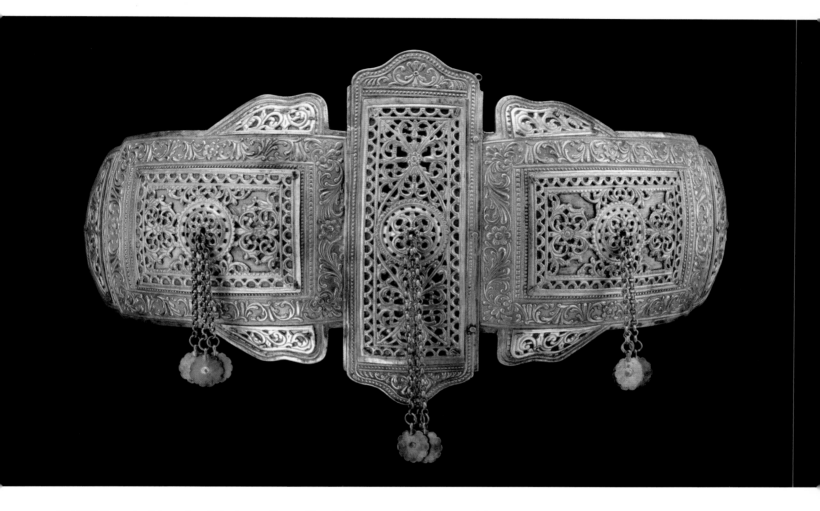

BUCKLE. *gulmish pafta.* Miyak, Smilevo, Demir Hisar municipality, c.1880.
A.2008.7.13V

Metal, gold wash, length 16 ½ in. (42 cm). The Ronald Wixman/Stephen Glaser
Collection.

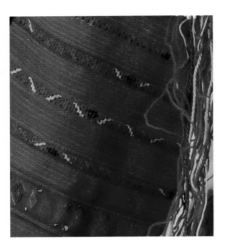

YOUNG WOMAN'S FESTIVAL DRESS. Miyak, Krushevo, c. 1880

Cotton, wool, metallic thread, metal, glass beads. Gift of Bernard W. Ziobro, The Ronald Wixman/Stephen Glaser Collection, Gift of the Macedonian Arts Council. About 10 miles north of Demir Hisar is the town of Krushevo; the village of Zheleznik lies between the two towns. As usual with Miyak dress, the dominant embroidery is on the sleeves and chest of the chemise. All the other needlework is couching or chain stitch. If a woman brought the right side point of the head scarf across her forehead and pinned it in place, she was telling the world that she was engaged. If she brought the front points forward over her shoulder, she signaled that there had been a death in her family. Either side or both sides in front of the shoulder denoted a different degree of familial closeness. Another version of the *glaina sokay* can be seen in the back view.

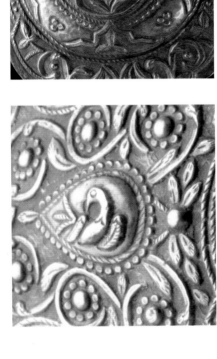

YOUNG WOMAN'S FESTIVAL DRESS. Miyak, Krushevo, c. 1880

OVERCOAT. *klashenik*. Miyak, Krushevo, c. 1880. A.2010.6.94

Wool, cotton, metallic thread, 37 x 10¾ in. (94 x 27 cm). Gift of Bernard W. Ziobro.
Vestigial sleeves are no longer useful; here they have shrunk to narrow flaps that
hang down the back. The wearer tucked these flaps into the belt, *prepashka,* where
they were not visible at all. Their appearance on outer garments, particularly for
men, harks back to ancient dress practices introduced to Europe from Central Asia.[8]

E. Knauer, "Toward a History of the Sleeved Coat," *Expedition 21*, no. 1 (1978): 18–36.

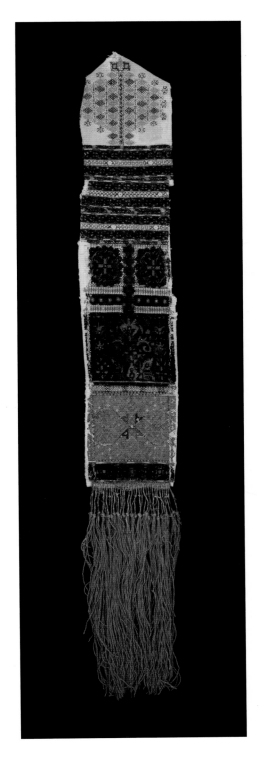
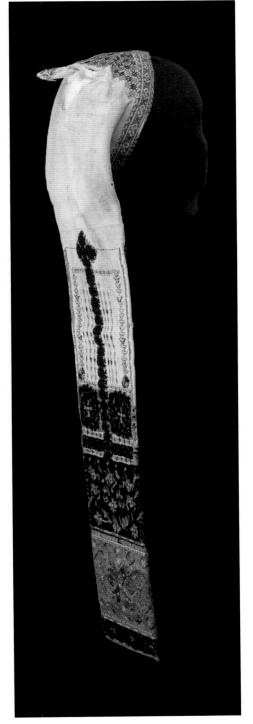

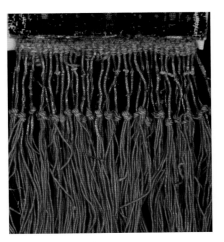

HEADPIECE. *sokay.* Strushko Pole, c. 1880. FA.2010.67.1

[Left] Linen or hemp, cotton, wool, silk, metal, 36 ¹³⁄₁₆ x 6 ½ in. (93.5 x 16.5 cm). Gift of DeWitt Mallary, IFAF Collection. The headpiece, *sokay,* was worn by a bride under the head scarf. Both of these show the older *nofteno* embroidery characteristic of the two areas, as well as the *sokaechko,* a type of straight stitch, and the horizontal stitch, *grabeno.* This example also has, unusually, several bands of drawn thread *kinatica.*

HEADPIECE. *sokay.* Strushki Drimkol, c. 1880. FA.2010.13.1

Linen or hemp, cotton, wool, silk, 35 ¾ x 5 ½ in. (91 x 14 cm). IFAF Collection. This *sokay* is missing its fringe, but the shaped cap is intact. Both *sokays* were woven with bast fiber warp and cotton weft, creating a mixed fabric. Not every family in a village owned a *sokay;* those who didn't would borrow one for a wedding.

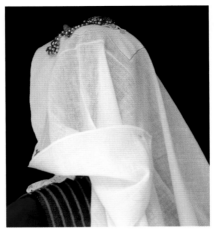

NEW BRIDE'S DRESS. Strushki Drimkol, c. 1920

[Details of Following Spread] Cotton, wool, metallic thread, glass beads, metal sequins. Gift of Blagorodna Josifovska. The strong similarities between this and the
new bride's ensemble from Ohridsko Pole reflect cultural and geographic proximity; the city of Ohrid is approximately eight miles from the town of Struga and
Strushki Drimkol. Some of the differences between the two illustrated are due to
age. For instance, the embroidery on the chemise would be in the relief stitch
nofteno (seen on the older *sokay* from the same area) instead of the cross stitch
seen here. The quilted cotton *zoban* with velvet front replaced the wool *klashenik*
in the twentieth century. At the turn of the twentieth century newly married
women wore a densely patterned and very long wool belt wrapped over the black
belt from the breasts to the hips and a more ornate belt with pompoms and coins
attached to it, later replaced by a simplified *kolan*. Separate velvet sleevelets and
the head scarf, *marama,* didn't change.

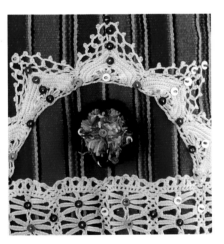

NEW BRIDE'S DRESS. Ohridsko Pole, c. 1910

Cotton, wool, metallic thread, metal, silk or synthetic, glass beads. Gift of Bernard W. Ziobro, Gift of the Macedonian Arts Council, IFAF Collection, Gift of Mr. and Mrs. William F. Hennessey. The Ohridsko Pole ensemble combines aspects of the Debar-Reka and Brsyak dress practices. The wide panels of embroidery on the sleeves and the embroidered collar and neck opening are similar to those of the Brsyak chemise, whereas the white drawn thread work on the bottom resembles that on the Miyak, Debarski Drimkol, and Golo Brdo chemises. On this garment, the white work is done with a different technique in which threads are removed from the cloth of the garment and replaced with needle-woven threads. The chemise is the oldest item of this group, dated c. 1880. Over it is a quilted cotton vest with velvet yoke and silver-gilt embroidery, *elek srmen,* and a wool sleeveless coat, *klashenik.* The separate upper sleevelets are velvet embroidered with silver-gilt thread and are called *r'kai kadifeni.* The head scarf, *marama,* is draped and pinned in place. The apron was probably more recently made than the other garments; the lace was probably added later still.

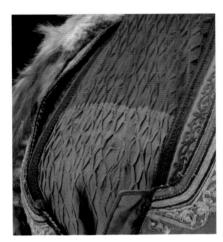

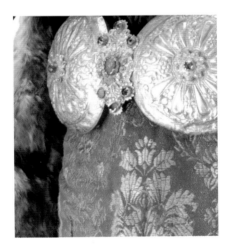

OVERCOAT. *djube.* Gorna Prespa, c. 1900. A.2010.23.1

Wool, fur, metallic thread, silk, 41 ⁵⁄₁₆ x 13 ¾ in. (105 x 35 cm). Gift of Mr. and Mrs. William F. Hennessey.

NEW BRIDE'S DRESS. Gorna Prespa, c.1900

[Details of Following Spread] Cotton, wool, fur, hide, metallic thread, silk, rayon, plastic buttons, glass beads and gems, metal, linen. Gift of Mr. and Mrs. William F. Hennessey, The Ronald Wixman/Stephen Glaser Collection. The bride's dress from Gorna Prespa is distinguished by the long black *djube* lined with fur and decorated with *srma* embroidery. Under it the bride wore an embroidered chemise, a smocked dickey, a white wool coat with velvet sleeves, a vest with silver-gilt embroidery, a long braided belt, a red-and black-striped wool apron, a silk brocade apron, *predsemnik,* and a large buckle. Gorna Prespa is located in the far south of Macedonia, near the borders of Greece and Albania. The ensemble shown here is very similar to what was worn in the town of Resen at the time.

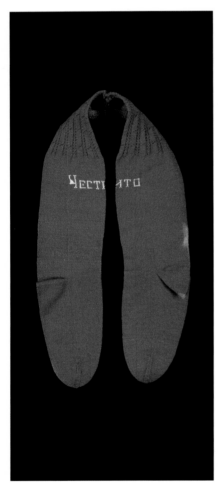

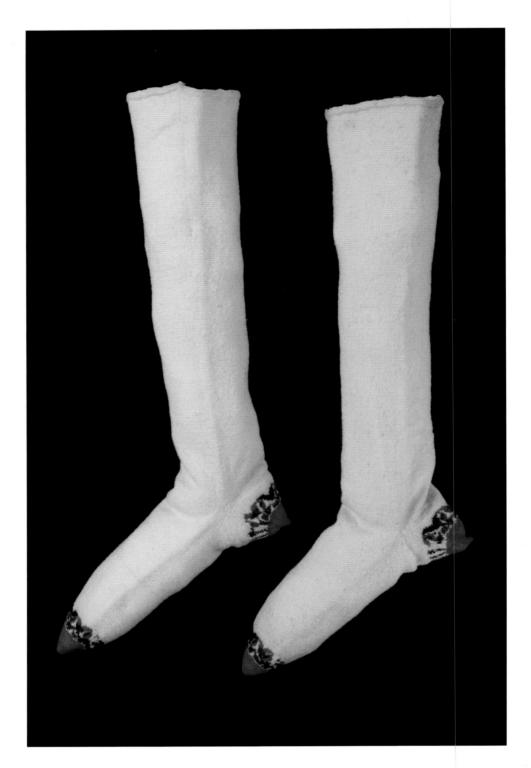

SOCKS. *chorabi*. Gorna Prespa, c.1900. A.2010.76.30ab

Wool, length 19 ⅝ in. (50 cm). Gift of the Macedonian Arts Council.

SOCKS. Gorna Prespa, c.1900. A.2010.23.10ab

Cotton, length 20 in. (51 cm). Gift of Mr. and Mrs. William F. Hennessey. Socks were knitted by the bride and given as a gift to her in-laws or guests at the wedding. They were worn by the guests around the neck. The word embroidered across the socks is "congratulations."

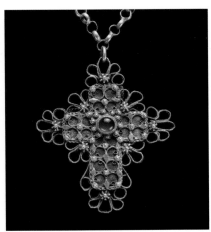

CROSS. *krst.* c.1900. FA.1969.43.14

Metal, glass, wood or paper, 2 ¾ x 2 ⅜ in. (7 x 6 cm). IFAF Collection.

CHEST ORNAMENT. *kustek topkayliya.* c.1890. A.1955.86.699/3137

Silver, glass, length 21½ in. (54.5 cm). Gift of Florence Dibell Bartlett. Men wore the silver *kustek* in the same manner as the beaded *kustek*. It was an urban rather than rural piece of jewelry, worn across the Ottoman Empire by wealthy men.

HAIR PINS. *igla.* c.1900. [Above left] A.2008.7.42 [Above right] FA.1969.43.16

Metal, glass, [Above left] length 5 ½ in. (14 cm). The Ronald Wixman/Stephen Glaser Collection. [Above right] length 5 ⅛ in. (13 cm). IFAF Collection. The word *igla* means pin and is also used to name the Miyak-type head ornament. The *igla* was worn in many parts of Macedonia.

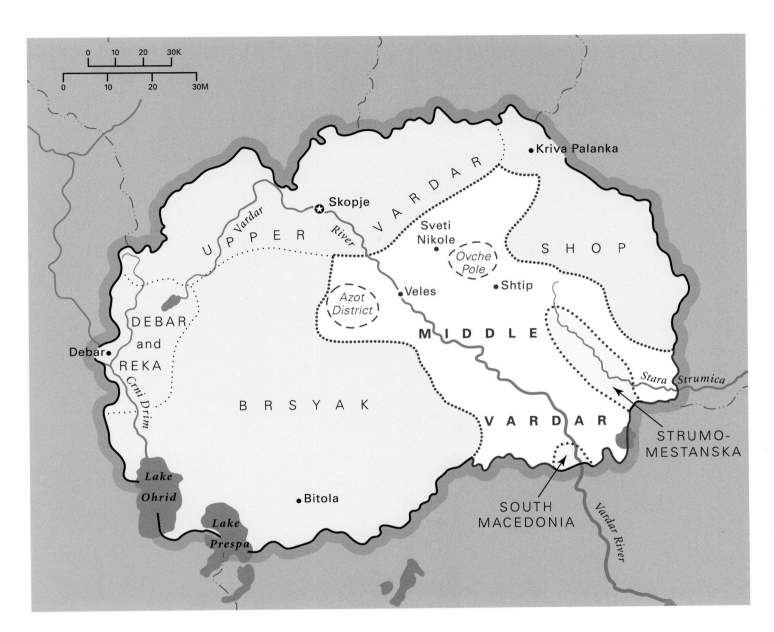

Middle Vardar

The Middle Vardar (Srednovardarska) region is not considered an ethnographic entity for general scholarly purposes but is classified as an ethnographic subgroup in the study of dress. It consists of a slice of the interior of the country on either side of the Vardar River, meeting the Upper Vardar on the north, the Shop on the east, the Brsyak on the west, and the South Macedonian region on the south. The relatively flat land is crossed by numerous rivers, making it suitable for intensive agriculture. The river valley has also provided an easy route for north-south travel since the second century BC, when the Romans built the Via Axios through it.

NEW BRIDE'S DRESS. Ovche Pole, c. 1920

Cotton, wool, metallic thread, paper, metal, rayon. Gift of Mr. Donald V. Berlanti.
Characteristic of the more eastern part of the country, this chemise has little embroidery, only a very narrow band of needlework on the edge of the sleeve. The
white dickey is called a *manta* here. A tailor constructed the red-striped *elek* in
an unusual fashion. After the fabric was woven, the tailor would cut it into shape,
stitch and gather each skirt piece, and then sew the pieces. This process created the
distinct crinkled texture needed for this garment. The soberly striped apron with
three very narrow bands of tiny woven motifs on each side was tied on over the patterned belt, *zunitsa*. The quilted black cotton velvet *minton* went over everything.
The bride and newly married woman wore a black scarf, *kalavatka;* unmarried girls
wore a white scarf on their heads. Older examples had more substantial needlework edging called *sorka,* similar to the Turkish *oya.* The woven scarf tucked into the
waist was essential; a newly married woman was not supposed to be seen on the
street without one.[9] Zdravev, *Folk Costumes,* 135.

YOUNG WOMAN'S FESTIVAL DRESS. Miyak, Azot district, c. 1920

Cotton, wool, metal, silk, glass, synthetic. Gift of Bernard W. Ziobro, Gift of the Macedonian Arts Council, The Ronald Wixman/Stephen Glaser Collection. By wearing this bridal chemise before the actual wedding, a young woman announced that she was engaged to be married. It's a bridal garment because the sleeves have drawn thread embroidery on them, a style of decoration not worn by unmarried girls. Miyaks in this part of Macedonia did not use silver-gilt thread or braid, but instead used yellow mercerized cotton thread for trim, seen here on the sleeves and the openings of the upper garments. Garments on this mannequin include a blouse, *mintan,* visible only as sleeve ends and blue and black trim on the chest, the bridal chemise, and the outermost garment of wool, *klashenik.* The apron, *kivchena skutina,* is covered by three scarves except for its bottom fringe. The ornamented belt with fringed ends, *prepashka,* is seen in the back view. A *pafta* and head scarf, *darpna,* complete the outfit.

246

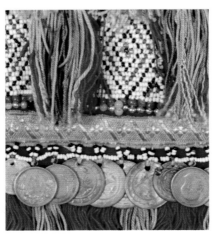

HEADPIECE. *sokay.* Miyak, Azot district, c.1920. A.2010.6.92

Wool, cotton, metal, glass beads, 49 x 19 ⅟₁₆ in. (124.5 x 50 cm). Gift of Bernard W. Ziobro. A bride wore the *sokay*. Older *sokay* from Azot district had more embroidery and fewer or no glass beads. There are Ottoman, Bulgarian, and Yugoslavian coins of different dates on this *sokay*.

Credits

CREDITS FOR FULL ENSEMBLES

Key:

DB	Donald Berlanti
WH	Mr. and Mrs. William F. Hennessey
IFAF	International Folk Art Foundation Collection
VJ	Vladimir Janevski
BJ	Blagorodna Josifovska
MAC	Macedonian Arts Council
MP	Museum Purchase
RW	Ronald Wixman/Stephen Glaser Collection
MZ	Mike Zafirovski
	in memory of his parents,
	Svetozar and Ljubica Zafirovski
Z	Bernard and Susan Ziobro

Excluding the IFAF Collection, all donations of pieces listed in these credits were made through the Macedonian Arts Council

1 **Skopska Blatiya**
   Wedding dress, c. 1910
IFAF Belt FA.1972.26.3d
      Necklace FA.2008.23.20
      Vest FA.1972.26.3b
MAC Paper Flowers A.2010.76.37
RW Apron A.2008.7.54
     Vest A.2008.7.52
Z Chemise A.2010.6.16
   Head Cover A.2010.6.19
   Jacket A.2010.6.21
Private Collection Head Belt

2 **Skopska Blatiya**
   Wedding dress, *crnetica*
IFAF Belt with srma FA.1972.26.1d
      Waist Towel FA.1972.26.2d
RW Chemise A.2008.7.51
     Neck Piece A.2008.7.25
Z Apron A.2010.6.11
   Belt A.2010.6.14
   Head Cloth A.2010.6.13
   Sleeveless Coat A.2010.6.10
   Vest A.2010.6.12

3 **Skopska Blatiya**
   Girl's dress
IFAF Apron FA.1996.66.14
      Belt FA.1996.66.15
      Chemise FA.1996.66.12
      Jacket FA.1996.66.13

4 **Skopska Blatiya**
   New groom's dress
IFAF Hat FA.1972.26.2f
      Shirt FA.1972.26.2b
      Shoes FA.1972.26.2h
      Socks FA.1972.26.2g
      Waist Scarf FA.1972.26.2d
WH Scarf A.2010.23.12
Z Belt A.2010.6.130
   Trousers A.2010.6.127
   Vest A.2010.6.129

5 **Zhegligovo**
   Wedding dress
MAC Beaded Belt A.2010.77.2
     Belt A.2010.76.27
     Chemise A.2010.76.26

Hat A.2010.76.25
Head Band A.2010.77.14
Head Scarf A.2010.77.13
Pin A.2010.77.4
Vest A.2010.76.28
MP Buckle A.2010.19.3v
Z Apron A.2010.6.133

6 **Karaguni Vlach**
   New bride's dress
IFAF Dickey FA.2008.23.1
      Hat FA.2010.63.1
      Long Jacket FA.2008.23.4
      Short Jacket FA.2008.23.3
MAC Apron A.2010.77.33
     Belt A.2010.77.34
     Jumper A.2010.77.30
     Head Band A.2010.77.32
     Head Scarf A.2010.77.31
     Sleeveless Coat A.2010.77.29

7 **Dolni Polog**
   New bride's dress
MAC Apron A.2010.76.5
     Blouse A.2010.76.6
     Cap A.2010.76.4
     Paper Flowers A.2010.76.35, .36
     Hair Ornaments A.2010.76.2ab
     Head Band A.2010.76.3
Z Apron A.2010.6.63
   Chemise A.2010.6.62
   Head Cover A.2010.6.65
   Jacket A.2010.6.140
   Vest A.2010.6.141

8 **Suva Gora**
   Young woman's festival dress
MAC Waist Scarf A.2010.77.15
RW Necklace A.2009.15.52
    Pin A.2008.7.42
Z Belt A.2010.6.72
   Blouse A.2010.6.73
   Chemise A.2010.6.71
   Coat A.2010.6.75
   Head Scarf A.2010.6.76
   Head Strap A.2010.6.77
   Large Apron A.2010.6.67
   Small Apron A.2010.6.66
   Vest A.2010.6.74

9   **Eastern Slavishte**
     New bride's dress
MAC Head Scarf A.2010.77.16
     Dickey A.2010.76.17
     Necklace A.2010.76.33
     Paper Flowers A.2010.76.37
Z   Apron A.2010.6.49
     Belt A.2010.6.53
     Chemise A.2010.6.52
     Coat A.2010.6.55
     Waist Towel A.2010.6.56

10   **Piyanets**
     New bride's dress
VJ   Apron A.2010.76.13
     Bag A.2010.76.16
     Belt A.2010.76.11
     Chemise A.2010.76.9
     Dickey A.2010.76.12
     Head Scarf A.2010.76.14
     Jacket A.2010.76.10
     Waist Towel A.2010.76.15
MAC Paper Flowers A.2010.76.37
MZ   Necklace A.2010.77.3
WH   Belt A.2010.23.15

11   **Miyak, Mala Reka**
     New bride's dress
MP   Head Jewelry A.2010.19.1
RW   Blouse A.2008.7.44
     Buckle A.2008.7.13v
     Coat A.2008.7.45
     Coin Belt A.2008.7.14
     Outer Sash A.2008.7.47
     Under Sash A.2008.7.48
     Vest A.2008.7.46
Z   Chemise A.2010.6.33
     Head Scarf A.2010.6.38
     Silk Apron A.2010.6.32
     Small Apron A.2010.6.31
     Waist Scarf A.2010.6.139

12   **Miyak**
     Young man's festival dress
IFAF Shoes FA.1972.26.1h
RW   Belt A.2009.15.4
     Hat A.2010.15.5
     Jacket A.2009.15.2

Pants A.2009.15.3
Shirt A.2009.15.1
Z   Overcoat A.2010.6.135

13   **Gorna Reka**
     Wedding dress
IFAF Apron FA.2008.23.15
     Belt FA.2008.23.9
     Blouse FA.2008.23.12
     Coat FA.2008.23.13
     Coin Belt FA.2008.23.16
     Head Cover FA.2008.23.18
     Vest FA.2008.23.8
     Sash FA.11972.26.2e
     Sash FA.2008.23.17
     Waist Scarf FA.2008.23.19
MZ   Chemise A.2010.76.7
     Hat with coins A.2010.76.8
WH   Waist Scarf, peach A.2010.23.14
     Waist Scarf, white A.2010.23.13

14   **Debarsko Pole**
     Wedding dress
MAC Chemise A.2010.76.32
     Waist Scarf A.2010.76.31
Z   Apron A.2010.6.43
     Belt A.2010.6.44
     Hat A.2010.6.46
     Head Cover A.2010.6.47
     Jacket A.2010.6.40
     Sleevelets A.2010.6.45
     Velvet Vest A.2010.6.41
     Vest A.2010.6.42

15   **Debarski Drimkol**
     New bride's dress
IFAF Vest FA.2010.52.2
Private Collection Hip Scarf
RW   Apron A.2009.15.47
     Chemise A.2009.15.45
     Dickey A.2009.15.49
     Head Scarf A.2009.15.48
     Under Jacket A.2008.7.57
WH   Scarf A.2010.23.11

16   **Golo Brdo**
     Wedding dress
IFAF Cross FA.1969.43.12a CE
MZ   Buckle A.2010.77.1

Necklace A.2010.77.5

RW Sash A.2008.7.62

Z Apron A.2010.6.23
Beaded Belt A.2010.6.28
Belt A.2010.6.24
Chemise A.2010.6.22
Dickey A.2010.6.138
Hat A.2010.6.29
Head Jewelry A.2010.6.27
Head Scarf A.2010.6.30
Jacket A.2010.6.25
Vest A.2010.6.7

17 **Gorni Bitolski Sela**
Wedding dress

IFAF Necklace FA.1972.26.1e

RW Apron A.2009.15.16
Belt A.2009.15.17
Buckle A.2008.7.38V
Dickey A.2008.7.2
Head Scarf A.2008.7.21
Jacket A.2009.15.15
Waist Jewelry A.2008.7.24

Z Chemise A.2010.6.57

18 **Gorni Bitolski Sela**
c. 1950 Wedding dress

RW Apron A.2009.15.33
Belt A.2009.15.34
Chemise A.2009.15.29
Dickey A.2009.15.31
Head Scarf A.2009.15.32
Jacket A.2009.15.30

19 **Bitolski Podmariovski Sela**
New bride's dress

RW Chemise A.2008.7.15
Coin Belt A.2009.15.7
Dickey A.2008.7.28
False Braid A.2008.7.22
Head Cover A.2008.7.37
Jacket A.2009.15.7
Sash A.2008.7.17

Z Apron A.2010.6.111

20 **Mariovo**
Wedding dress

RW Apron A.2008.7.31
Apron Jewelry A.2008.7.41

Chemise A.2008.7.27
Coin Belt A.2008.7.38v
Head Scarf A.2008.7.36
Jewelry: chains with coins
A.2008.7.39
A.2008.7.40
A.2008.7.41
Medallions with coins
A.2008.7.65v
A.2009.15.53v

Z Belt A.2010.6.124
Buckle A.2010.6.86v
Dickey A.2010.6.144
Head Cover A.2010.6.122
Overcoat, cotton A.2010.6.119
Overcoat, wool A.2010.6.118
Sleevelets A.2010.6.123v
Waist Scarf A.2010.6.126

21 **Prilepsko Pole**
New bride's dress

RW Belt A.2008.7.38v
Belt, black wool A.2008.7.19
A.2008.7.32
Buckle A.2008.7.23
Chemise A.2009.15.6
Jacket A.2009.15.7
Jewelry: chains with coins
A.2008.8.39
A.2009.15.12
A.2008.7.66
Narrow Sash with coins A.2009.15.51
Wide Sash with coins A.2009.15.11v

WH Waist Scarves A.2010.23.11 and 12

Z Apron A.2010.6.80
Belt, black wool A.2010.6.124
Head Cover A.2010.6.85
Neck Piece A.2010.6.84
Sleevelets A.2010.6.81v
Vest A.2010.6.79

22 **Kicheviya**
Wedding dress (both images)

RW Apron A.2009.15.42
Chemise A.2009.15.36
Dickey A.2008.7.1
Head Scarf A.2009.15.39
Hood A.2009.15.4
Jacket A.2009.15.37

Jacket A.2009.15.41
Waist Jewelry A.2009.15.13

23 **Miyak, Smilevo**
Wedding dress
IFAF Buckle FA.2010.52.1
MAC Waist Scarf A.2010.77.8
RW Apron A.2008.7.6
Blouse A.2008.7.4
Chemise A.2008.7.11
Head Scarf A.2008.7.10
Head Jewelry A.2008.7.12
Jacket A.2008.7.3
Sash A.2008.7.7
Scarf A.2008.7.9
Vest A.2008.7.5

24 **Miyak, Krushevo**
Young woman's festival dress
MAC Waist Scarf A.2010.77.12
RW Buckle A.2008.7.50v
Z Apron A.2010.6.97
Chemise A.2010.6.93
Head Piece A.2010.6.99
Head Scarf A.2010.6.142
Sash A.2010.6.96
Sleeveless Coat A.2010.6.94
Vest A.2010.6.95

25 **Strushki Drimkol**
New bride's dress
BJ Apron A.2010.77.24
Beaded Belt A.2010.77.25
Belt A.2010.77.39
Blouse A.2010.77.19
Chemise A.2010.77.20
Head Jewelry A.2010.77.28
Head Scarf A.2010.77.28
Scarf with pompoms A.2010.77.26
Sleevelets A.2010.77.22ab
Vest A.2010.77.21

26 **Ohridsko Pole**
New bride's dress
IFAF Necklace with cross FA.1969.43.14
MAC Belts A.2010.77.38 and 39
Head Jewelry A.2010.77.35
Vest A.2010.77.36

WH Waist Scarf A.2010.23.11
Z Apron A.2010.6.104
Chemise A.2010.6.100
Head Scarf A.2010.6.102
Sleeveless Coat A.2010.6.100
Sleevelets A.2010.6.103

27 **Gorna Prespa**
New bride's dress
RW Buckle A.2009.15.11v
WH Belt A.2010.23.8
Chemise A.2010.23.1
Coat A.2010.23.4
Dickey A.2010.23.9
Head Scarf A.2010.23.7
Silk Apron A.2010.23.3
Sleeveless Coat A.2010.23.1
Vest A.2010.23.6
Wool Apron A.2010.23.2

28 **Ovche Pole**
New bride's dress
DB Apron A.2010.77.18
Belt A.2010.77.17
Black Head Scarf A.2010.76.23
Chemise A.2010.76.18
Dickey A.2010.76.19
Flowers A.2010.76.34 and 37
Jacket A.2010.76.24
Necklace A.2010.76.33
Peach Head Scarf A.2010.76.22
Vest A.2010.76.20
Waist Scarf A.2010.76.21

29 **Miyak, Azot district**
Young woman's festival dress
MAC Blouse A.2010.77.9
Head Scarf A.2010.77.8
Waist Scarves A.2010.77.10ab
RW Buckle A.2008.7.23V
Z Apron A.2010.6.91
Belt A.2010.6.89
Chemise A.2010.6.87
Head Cover A.2010.6.90
Sleeveless Coat A.2010.6.87

Glossary

EDITOR'S NOTE: The glossary should include all the Macedonian words used in the text as well as a few others. Variations of spelling and words from different regions are arranged as logically and helpfully as possible. Words are not identified by region. Many thanks to Bernard Ziobro for helping proof this.

WOMEN'S GARMENTS

Bokchenitsa, bovcha: apron
Chevre: head scarf
Chultar: wedding apron
Chultsi, kaltsi, shutarke, tozlutzi: footless socks
Darkma: head scarf with embroidery and tassel
Darpna: embroidered and fringed head scarf
Distimeli: head scarf
Dizgiya: woven belt or sash
Fusta: wool undergarment
Futa, vuta: apron
Glaina: braid holder
Gornik, gornenik, gornitsa, zgornik: sleeveless wool coat
Gradnik, grlo, keptar, manta, parti: dickey
Guna: overcoat with or without fringe on sides
K'chula: bridal hat
K'ndusha: pleated sleeveless coat
Kalavatka: head scarf
Kalemkyar: printed head scarf
Kaltsi, kaltzi: knitted wristlets
Kapa, fez, fesche: cap, hat
Kavrak: head band rolled from head scarf
Klashenik: sleeveless wool coat, can have vestigial sleeves
Kmesha: chemise
Kolan: belt
Kolanche: small belt
Korpa: head scarf
Koshula: chemise, long shirt
Koshulche: blouse worn under the chemise
Krpa, krpche: head scarf
Kusale: short wool vest
Kutacha: apron
Kyurdiya: sleeveless wool coat
Libade: long sleeved jacket
Marama: head scarf
Minton, mintan: long sleeve blouse
Naniz: decorated red print pointed hip scarves
Peshkir, pestar: apron
Poala: apron
Predsemnik: apron
Pregaca, pregach, opregach, apron
Pregrlak: jacket
Rakavchinya, rakajchine, rakavchunya, r'kai, rakavi: upper arm sleevelets
Remen, remenche: head strap
Resachka: sleeveless wool coat with fringe inside
Sagiya: sleeveless cotton coat
Saya: fitted vest worn by bride

Shamiya: head or waist scarf
Shayak: coat
Shkepa: head scarf
Shopska bokcha: apron
Skutacha, skutina, skutinche, skutnik: apron
Sokay, sokaj, sokai, glavinka: head cover
Stramnik: towel tucked into the waist
Stranitsi: pair of print hip scarves
Telena dilyka: apron
Torba: pocket purse
Tresalina: wristlets with lace and beads
Tulben: turban or head scarf
Ubrus, obrus: bridal head cover
Zavelyika, zaviatchka: apron
Zoban, zubun, z'ban, zobanche: short-sleeved or sleeveless wool coat
Zunitsa: woven belt

MEN'S GARMENTS

Ayta, ayti: shirt
Bechvi, betchve: wool trousers
Dizghii: garters for the socks
Dzhamadan: man's vest
Fustan: man's upper garment with many gores to make a full skirt
Gakyi, gatyi: trousers
Keche: pill box hat
Kepe: short wool jacket
Mintan: shirt
Nazovtzi, tozlutsi: wool puttees
Shubara: black sheepskin hat
V'stan, v'stanica: gored shirt

UNISEX GARMENTS

Chorabi, kalchini, kolchini, perpoci: socks
Dolama: long sleeved, pleated overcoat
Dzhube, djube, jube: sleeveless wool over-garment,
  fitted at the upper part with full skirt
Elek, eleche, jelek, yelek: waistcoat or vest,
  waist length for men, below hip and wider for women
Klashenik: sleeveless wool outer garment
Kyurdiya: sleeveless over garment
Opinci, opanci: leather shoes
Poyas, pojas, posh: belt
Prepashka: wide sash w/fringe
Ruchnitsi: towels worn over the shoulder or in the belt
Saya, sagiya: cotton or linen sleeveless outer garment
Torba: woven bag

PARTS OF GARMENTS INCLUDING
WHERE EMBROIDERY IS PLACED

Bochnitsi: gores on bottom sides of chemise
Boyov, bojov, bojovi: vertical panels of embroidery on the back of a chemise
Dolnitsata: bottom edge of chemise
Gugan: the embroidered decoration on one corner of the head scarf darkma
Okolno: embroidered border on hem of chemise
Partite: border of neck and front opening on chemise
Prednipoli, prednitsa: front of upper garment
Rakaj, rakavi, r'kai: sleeve
Ratkavitsi, rokavi: vestigal sleeves
Zadnipoli, zadnica: back of upper garment
Zatilok, koril, jache: collar of chemise

MOTIFS

Arbalii: flat diamonds
Bayraci: flags
Cvekyinya, tsvekyinya: floral motifs
Glavki: heads, circles
Gradenica: fence line
Granka: branch
Krstovi, krst: cross
Loza: hooks or spirals around vetki
Lozi: vines
Mashko petle: cockerel, shaped like a tiny diamond with extended sides
Mechkina dira: bear's paw print
Pauni: peacock
Petanek: eight sided star
Piltsi: chicks
Pobochnik porebornik: several circles that are stacked
Pratoi: columns of embroidery
Provezi: stacked diamonds
Uskolena: blocks of embroidery on bottom of chemise
Uskuknyak: triangular shapes
V'chkata traga: wolf's paw print
Vetka: oval shape on head scarf
Viyulka: swastika
Vrteshka: sun
Yagupovi pilinya: pullet or young hen
Zhelykorka: turtle
Zobalki: nine grapes

TRIMS

Bukme: yellow silk or cotton braid
Burmi: black braid, commercially made
Gaitan: braid
Kiska: fringe

Kitki: wool pompoms
Klabodan: silver-gilt thread
Monistra: bead
Oya, sorka, cucki: crocheted or needlework trim
Pulyeki, puljaki: sequins
Srma, serma, sermena, harsafi: silver-gilt thread and embroidery

TECHNIQUES

Chikme: needle lace, white work on side gores, drawn thread
Grabeno: horizontal straight stitch
Kinatica, kinatitsa: drawn thread
Krvchinya: cross stitch
Kyesme: drawn thread
Lozeno, crneto, orano: double running or Holbein stitch
Naklavano: relief outline
P'lnatica: slanted Slav stitch, Miyak dialect
Pisanechko: back stitch
Pisano: satin stitch
Podlachno: vertical straight stitch
Polnez, polnezh, orano: oblique or slanted Slav stitch
Poplit, poplitz: single needle technique, looks like knitting
Skortsi, nofteno: raised or three dimensional stitch
Travtsi, tegli, or *sindzhati:* outline stitch
Trepit: chain stitch
Trupa: double sided or reversible stitch
Zaorok, zalozok, and *zavez:* samplers

MATERIALS

Aladzha, anteriya: red, pinstriped, wool fabric
Kazmir: fine, commercially produced wool fabric
Kenarliya: striped cotton cloth used sometimes for chemise
Saya: heavy cotton cloth
Shayak, shaak, sha'ak, klashna: fulled wool cloth

JEWELRY AND ORNAMENTS

Amuri: beaded hat band
Brno di mrsyali: beaded belt
Chelnik: forehead ornament
Gyerdan, ledenik, panzur, rzhonde: fish scale coin chest ornament
Gyerdan: neck piece
Igla: hair pin, also three strand head jewelry
Kishka: beaded triangular head ornament
Kiska: strands of beads hung from a braid, tassel, fringe
Kitki: hair ornament pins
Kocel, kotsel, prtzle: black braided yarn attached to the shoulders or waist
Kolanche: small beaded belt

Krst: Cross or ornament with cross design
Kustek, kyustek: silver or beaded chest or waist jewelry
 worn by both men and women
Nizalka: coin belt
Pafta, pafti: belt buckle
Shikoy: hairpins
Skopetz: chains with coins attached
Tas, tepelak, tepeluk, tepelik: metal disk for top of head
Tontuzi: imitation coins
Ushnitsi: earrings

OTHER TERMS

Alena, alova, brozdena, chista, gyuvezna: shades of red
Belo: white
Crna: black
Jatak: weft
Kyulavka: horn, as in the horn shape
 of the front of the bridal head cover, horned god
 or goddess representing fertility in old cult
Mladozhenya: bridegroom
Nevesta: bride
Nevestinska: bridal
Nevestinstovo: first year after the wedding
Pashkari: cards for preparing wool and cotton
Rozova, pembe: pink
Zholt: yellow

Biographies

SANJA DIMOVSKA graduated in ethnology from the University in Belgrade in 1990 and works in the Museum of Macedonia as a curator for folk and urban dress since 1991. She curated the exhibition of urban dress in Macedonia *Ala Turka–Ala Franga*, as well as *Wedding Stockings* and co-curated *From the Ottoman Traditions in Macedonia* in Istanbul. She has participated in the work of international scientific conferences in Macedonia and Turkey and has published articles in those countries. Her major interest is urban dress, particularly the Oriental type of dress, embroidery and lace. She is co-author of the article on the urban dress in Macedonia for the Berg Encyclopedia of World Dress and Fashion. She participated in the project *Sharing the Same Taste* organized by the national committees of UNESCO for Turkey and Macedonia.

TATJANA GORGIOSKA graduated in ethnology from the Skopje University in 1993, where she got her MA degree in 2006. Since 1993 she works as a curator in the Department of Ethnology at Museum of the City of Skopje, in charge of the collections for urban dress and household items. She has curated or co-curated several exhibition in Museum of the City of Skopje including *Cultural Identity of the City of Skopje from 1945 up to the 1970s, The Most Beautiful —Wedding Dress from the 19th Century until Today, Material and Spiritual Culture of Macedonian Muslims, Mardi Gras Celebration in Skopje, Ethnical Variety in Skopje, The Fenix Trail,* and *Macedonia in 1913, Autochromes,* with Musée Départemental Albert Kahn, Boulogne, France. She is co-author of the monograph *Life in Skopje 1918–1941,* as well as of the article on Macedonian urban dress for the Berg Encyclopedia of World Dress and Fashion.

SLAVICA HRISTOVA is a senior curator in the Department of Ethnology at the Museum of the City of Skopje, in charge of collections of folk dress, pottery, and glass, since 1993. She has curated or co-curated several exhibitions: *Mardi Gras in Skopje, Material and Spiritual Culture of Macedonian Muslims, The Most Beautiful—Wedding Dress from the 19th Century until Today,* and *Cultural Identity of the City of Skopje from 1945 up to 1970s.* She is co-author of the monographs *Life in Skopje 1918–1941* and *Govrlevo Will Not Die,* and the article on Macedonian urban dress in the Berg Encyclopedia of World Dress and Fashion. She has published articles on formation and protection of ethnological collections, folk dress, symbols and beliefs in material culture, and contemporary subculture among young people. In 2006 she got her MA degree in ethnology at the Institute of Ethnology and Anthropology, Saints Cyril and Methodius University in Skopje.

VLADIMIR JANEVSKI holds a Master of Arts in ethnochoreology from Saints Cyril and Methodius University and presently teaches at the College for Music at the University Gotse Delchev in Shtip. He has lectured extensively at seminars and ethnological gatherings throughout Europe and worked as a researcher-curator of several private collections throughout Macedonia. He was recently awarded the Macedonian Ethnological Society's prize for his efforts to popularize ethnology in

Macedonia. He is a member of UNESCO's International Dance Council and of the Macedonian Ethnological Society. His most recent publication was as co-author of the article on Macedonian ethnic dress in the Berg Encyclopedia of World Dress and Fashion.

ANGELINA KRSTEVA graduated from the Department of Ethnology at Saints Cyril and Methodius University in Skopje and started working as an assistant for the Department of Traditional Textile Ornaments at the Folklore Institute in Skopje. From 1963 to 1965, she worked as a curator-ethnologist at the Museum of the City of Skopje, after which she received a position at the Museum of Macedonia as a curator-counselor for the Ethnological Department, where she worked until her retirement in 1982. Her main interests are traditional textile ornaments and traditional dress. She curated many thematic museum exhibitions both in Macedonia and abroad. She has also published over forty articles in various ethnological journals, as well as books on traditional embroidery, techniques, and dress. In 1976, she received the renowned prize of the city of Skopje "13 Noemvri" (13 November) for the album called *Macedonian Traditional Embroidery*. She remains rather active even after her retirement.

JASEMIN NAZIM is a curator of Traditional Textiles at the Museum of Macedonia in Skopje, Department of Ethnology, since 1982. She has curated and co-curated several exhibitions including the *Ethnology of Macedonia*–permanent exhibition in the Museum of Macedonia; *Copper Vessels and Kilims,* as well as *From the Ottoman Tradition of Macedonia* in the Museum of Turkish and Islamic Art in Istanbul and *Macedonian Wedding Kilims* in Toronto and New York. She has published a number of articles on the textile collection in the Museum of Macedonia, particularly on kilims, archaic types of Balkan textiles, and rush mats regarding especially their history from the Middle Ages until present. She has also researched the history of food in Macedonia.

BOBBIE SUMBERG received an MA and Ph.D from the University of Minnesota, Department of Design, Housing, and Apparel. Research for both these degrees in textile studies was conducted in West Africa. She currently holds the position of curator of Textiles and Costume at the Museum of International Folk Art in Santa Fe, New Mexico and has curated several exhibits including *Needles and Pins: Textiles and Tools, Dream On Beds from Asia to Europe,* and *Dressing Up: Children's Clothes from Around the World*. She recently authored the book *Textiles: Collection of the Museum of International Folk Art* and is co-author of *Sleeping Around: The Bed from Antiquity to Now*. She has published articles on dress and textiles of Nigeria and Côte d'Ivoire and on ethnic dress as well as research on the museum collection.

DAVORIN TRPESKI holds a Masters in ethnology (2005) and Ph.D in ethnology (2010) from the Institute of Ethnology and Anthropology at Saints Cyril and Methodius University in Skopje. He has contributed to several international projects concerning the interpretation of cultural heritage in Macedonia and South-East Europe. Currently, he is assistant professor at the Saints Cyril and Methodius University in the fields of political anthropology and anthropology of cultural heritage.

Colophon

THIS FIRST EDITION of *Young Brides, Old Treasures: Macedonian Embroidered Dress* is limited to 1,500 copies. Studio photography was done by Addison Doty. Historic photographs by Kurt Hielscher, c. 1920. Photographs of hair braiding by Vladimir Janevski. All poems and songs translated by Pavlina Proevska. The maps were created by Deborah Reade. Pre-press work was completed by Peter Ellzey. The book was designed by Arlyn Eve Nathan. The typefaces used were Minion, designed by Robert Slimbach in 1990 and Univers, designed by Adrian Frutiger in 1954. This book was printed in Dallas, Texas by Taylor Specialty Books.